How to Use This Book

This book is designed to be carried with you and to be used as a quick reference as you research, draft, revise, edit, and document sources in your written papers. Here's how to find topics you need:

1. Consult the **Quick Reference Guide** on the inside front cover of the book. This Guide can help you locate the section and chapter number of the topic you need.

2. For a more complete breakdown of the contents of the book, see the **Expanded Contents** on the inside back cover. The Expanded Contents provides a listing of the topics covered in each chapter.

3. Use the **Index** at the back of the book to locate a specific term that you want to find.

4. The blue **tabs** at the top of each page indicate the chapter and section number on that page.

5. **Running heads** at the top of each page indicate the topic covered on a particular page.

6. **Boldface terms** are defined in the text and in the Glossary.

7. **Web links** provide addresses for important writing resources on the Internet.

8. **Subsection numbers** identify specific topics within a section.

9. **Examples** illustrate the main points explained in the text.

10. **Cross-references** direct you to related information elsewhere in the text.

The New Century Pocket Guide for Writers

CHRISTINE A. HULT
Utah State University

THOMAS N. HUCKIN
University of Utah

PEARSON
Longman

New York Boston San Francisco
London Toronto Sydney Tokyo Singapore Madrid
Mexico City Munich Paris Cape Town Hong Kong Montreal

Senior Vice President, Publisher, and Acquisitions Editor: Joseph Opiela
Senior Development Editor: Judith Fifer
Executive Marketing Manager: Tamara Wederbrand
Production Manager: Donna DeBenedictis
Project Coordination, Text Design, and Electronic Page Makeup: Nesbitt Graphics, Inc.
Cover Design Manager: Wendy Ann Fredericks
Cover Designer: Kay Petronio
Cover Photo: Harvey Lloyd/FPG
Manufacturing Buyer: Lucy Hebard
Printer and Binder: RR Donnelley and Sons Company/Crawfordsville
Cover Printer: Coral Graphic Services, Inc.

Library of Congress Cataloging-in-Publication Data

Hult, Christine A.
    The new century pocket guide for writers/Christine A. Hult, Thomas
N. Huckin.
        p. cm.
Includes index.
    ISBN 0-321-09460-3
    1. English language—Rhetoric—Handbooks, manuals, etc. 2. English
language—Grammar—Handbooks, manuals, etc. 3. Report
writing—Handbooks, manuals, etc. I. Huckin, Thomas N. II. Title.
PE1408.H689 2004
808'.042—dc22

                                                                2003060630

Please visit our website at http://www.ablongman.com/hult

ISBN 0-321-09460-3

1 2 3 4 5 6 7 8 9 10—DOC—06 05 04 03

CHAPTER **1**

Drafting and Revising

Novice and experienced writers tend to devote different amounts of time and attention to preparing to write. Novice writers often dive right into drafting a final version of their paper. Rather than experimenting, inventing, and planning, they spend most of their time struggling with the writing itself. Many experienced writers, however, spend a great deal of time thinking about what

WEBLINK

http://web.uvic.ca/wguide/ Pages/StartHere.html

An introduction to various elements of the writing process

they want to say before they actually begin to write. Learn from these experienced writers—take time to prepare prior to drafting.

Your computer can help you with all stages of the writing process. You will learn different tips and techniques for composing and revising throughout this chapter.

1a Invent and prewrite

Writing begins with thinking. The words that appear on your computer screen are the result of the thinking you do prior to and during the writing process. In the prewriting stage, you invent or discover what you want to say about your subject. As the words *invent* and *discover* imply, during this period you delve into your subject, come up with new ideas, connect these new ideas with prior experiences and knowledge, read about and research your subject, and generally allow your thoughts to take shape.

1 Brainstorming

Brainstorming refers to generating random ideas or fragments of thought about a topic. You are probably familiar with brainstorming from writing classes you have taken in the past. It is possible to brainstorm as a group, call-ing out ideas to the instructor, who writes them on the blackboard; at a com-puter, either individually or with another classmate; or in your writing journal.

2 Freewriting

Freewriting is related to brainstorming in that it involves writing down thoughts as they come to mind. However, unlike brainstorming, freewriting is typically formulated in connected sentences rather than lists. The idea is to write rapidly in an informal style without conscious regard to details of us-age, spelling, and punctuation. It is possible to freewrite with pen and paper or at the computer. Using either your word-processing program or a writing journal, you can freewrite on a topic to generate ideas and to discover infor-mation stored in your mind.

3 Invisible writing

Invisible writing is a computer freewriting technique designed to release you from the inhibitions created by seeing your own words on the computer screen. Compulsive revisers find it difficult to ignore the errors they see on the screen and so are unable to write freely at the computer. When you write in-visibly, your words do not appear on the screen, so you are free to generate ideas without interruption. You can concentrate on the emerging thoughts rather than on the form those thoughts are taking.

4 Clustering

Clustering is a prewriting technique that can help you to see relationships among the ideas you have generated in brainstorming or freewriting exer-cises. You begin a clustering session by putting your topic, in the form of a word or a phrase, in the middle of a sheet of paper. Then, attach to your topic other words or phrases that come to mind, linking and connecting related ideas or subtopics. When you cluster, you free associate from one word or phrase to another, allowing your mind to trigger related ideas that may not have occurred to you before.

5 Debating

Debating is a prewriting technique that can help you to explore a controversial issue from all sides. You might begin by writing down all the generalizations you can think of about the topic—either handwriting them in your journal or typing them into a computer file.

If you generate your lists of generalizations using a word-processing program, you can add to, delete, replace, and rearrange the information. The general statements and evidence you accumulate while debating the topic can be used to start an outline or an exploratory draft of your paper.

1b Gather information

Particularly if your assignment is to write a research paper, you will need to supplement whatever prewriting techniques you use with information gathered from external sources. The ideas you read about and formulate will lead you into a more systematic and extensive search that is focused on a specific topic. If your writing task involves a significant research component, refer to Chapters 2, 3, and 4 for guidance.

There are several informal ways you can begin to gather information for your paper. You can discuss your ideas with classmates, friends, family members, and professors, who may be able to provide you with information. Browsing through periodicals in the current periodicals section of your library will tell you whether your topic is currently under discussion in the media. Or, you can use a search engine to browse the Internet, trying out a variety of keywords and subjects. As you begin your informal, preliminary research on a topic, you will also want to begin taking notes.

1c Develop and refine your thesis

Once you have explored your topic, done some prewriting, and consulted a few sources, you are ready to begin thinking about a logical order in which to present the ideas you have developed. No matter how good your information, if your paper is not organized, your readers will not be able to understand what you are trying to say.

1 Narrowing your focus

Through prewriting, you develop an awareness of what you know and do not know about a topic. As you look back at your prewriting, think about ways in which you could narrow your topic to a manageable size. Try to write down in one sentence what you take to be your specific, narrow topic.

2 Formulating a working thesis statement

Once you have written down your narrow topic, try to state in one or two sentences the main point you want to make about that topic. This will be your working thesis statement. A *thesis statement* concisely identifies the topic and main point of a piece of writing.

3 Evaluating and revising your working thesis

You may need to revise your working thesis several times as you draft your paper. This is why it is called a "working thesis": it can be clarified, modified, or even completely rewritten during the course of your writing process. Allow your thesis to evolve with your understanding of the topic.

4 Organizing your information

There is no one right way to organize material. The most frequently used organizational patterns are chronological (by *time*) and logical (*step-by-step*).

5 Writing an outline

Once you have decided which organizational pattern best suits your working thesis, you may find it useful to construct an outline for your paper. You need not be overly concerned with formal outline structure at this point, unless your teacher stipulates a particular outline format. An outline should serve as a guide as you write—not a constraint that confines and limits your thinking.

1d Review

When composing your first draft, you use the information and ideas you generated in your prewriting, as well as your working thesis and outline. In the composing stage of the writing process, your concern shifts from experimenting with ideas and gathering information to expanding your ideas and structuring them into effective, coherent prose. Review that crucial prewriting information before you begin composing your first draft.

1 Reviewing your thesis and outline

Next, review your working thesis and outline. Add any new ideas you discovered while reading through your prewriting. If you think the main idea has shifted since you wrote your working thesis, rewrite it and adjust your outline accordingly.

2 Using multiple windows

If you prefer, you can use your prewriting and outline documents for reference and begin composing from scratch in a new document. The WINDOW feature of many word-processing programs allows you to work on two or more documents simultaneously. Multiple windows are useful for keeping track of your ideas as you work—you can keep your prewriting, your outline, and your draft in separate windows. It is also possible to use separate windows to display different parts of your document at the same time. For example, you could insert your thesis into one window and your draft into another.

1e Draft

When you are ready to begin composing, you can choose from a number of different approaches. Two possible approaches are the building-block technique and the top-down method.

1 Using the building-block technique

One approach to composing is to create a group of building blocks that you can use to construct your text a piece at a time. Many writers first compose a skeleton of the finished text and then expand it by adding new arguments, supporting examples and evidence, or illustrative details: the "building blocks" of a text. Word processing is particularly effective for this approach. Some writers like to write their central paragraphs—the middle blocks of a text—first and add the introductory blocks and concluding paragraphs later. You can decide which blocks will be easiest and write those blocks first, saving the more difficult parts for last.

2 Using the top-down method

As an alternative to composing from building blocks, you may prefer to work from the beginning of your paper straight through to the end, thus moving from the top down. You can use your working thesis statement and the corresponding organizational plan to compose in this way. Type or COPY and PASTE your working thesis statement into a new document. With the thesis statement at the top of your screen, begin writing your draft, following the blueprint suggested by your thesis. Remember, your working thesis is just that—working. You can revise it at any time.

3 Avoiding writer's block

Each writer develops his or her own writing rhythms. It is a good idea to get into the habit of stopping a writing session when you know what comes next; this makes it easier to pick up where you left off when you are ready to continue. However, if you find yourself "blocked" as a writer, set your work aside for a few hours or even a few days. Get up and stretch, grab a cup of coffee or a soft drink before returning to your draft. Do not expect perfection from a first draft. Remember that writing is essentially rewriting; everything you write should undergo extensive revision in a continuous cycle of writing, revising, editing, and writing again.

1f   Collaborate

As you compose, you might find it helpful to collaborate with others, either face to face or via a computer network. In college classes, as in the work force, writers often work on projects in writing groups or writing teams. Your teammates can serve as a sounding board for your ideas and arguments.

1 Working with a group

Working with a group may be something you enjoy or something you dread, depending on whether your prior experience with group projects was positive or negative. In some group projects, one or two students may end up feeling that they are doing all the work. In other group projects, a few students may be bossy or controlling rather than cooperative. But if you pay attention to group dynamics and role assignments from the start of your collaborative project, you should do just fine.

2 Writing collaboratively

Once you have come up with an overall plan of action for your writing project, you can assign specific tasks or roles to group members. In one writing class, each group was assigned the task of developing a Web site on a topic related to cyberspace. The students in each group brainstormed together possibilities for their site, first deciding on the nature of the content their Web site would present and the audience it would address. They agreed to each write independently a two- to three-page piece that would be incorporated as a page at the site. Then, they assigned each person in the group a specific role, from site Webmaster to site publisher. Because each student knew exactly what his or her contribution would be, group members were able to work together cooperatively.

3 Collaborating via network

If you are involved in a joint writing project, forming an email discussion group can facilitate collaboration with others in the group. Students collaborating to write material for a Web site they were creating, for example, used a study group address so that they could email the first draft of each Web page to the entire writing group for review. Most email software offers the option INCLUDE EMAIL MESSAGE IN REPLY. That option places the entire message—in this case, the draft of a Web page—into the reply window. Members of the writing group could add their comments and suggestions in capital letters or italics to make them stand out from the draft itself. Then, by selecting the REPLY TO ALL option, they could send the reply message to everyone in the group, or, by selecting the REPLY TO SENDER option, they could send their reply to only the writer.

You can also use the email software's ATTACHMENT capability to facilitate collaboration with a writing group. This feature allows you to include a document (file) with the email message. In this way, you can send your actual word-processing document to the others in the group for their review. Group members can use the word-processing program's COMMENT feature (found in the INSERT menu) to insert their comments and suggestions for revisions. The paper and the comments can then be sent back to the writer, again as an email attachment.

1g Revise

Critical reading can highlight problems of focus, coherence, organization, development, tone, and formatting in your paper. Revising involves the tasks of adding to the text, deleting from the text, and rearranging information within the text to fix those problems. Using a word-processing program makes these tasks easy; knowing what to add, delete, and rearrange is the tricky part.

1 Revising for focus

Revisit your working thesis, and revise it to more accurately reflect the overall point of your text. Then revise each paragraph to ensure that it is focused on only one idea, which supports the thesis. Delete any paragraphs that are not related to the thesis.

WEBLINK

http://www.rpi.edu/web/writingcenter/revise.html

A list of eighteen revision tips and strategies

2 Revising for coherence

Wherever you notice that sentences do not flow smoothly in your draft, add appropriate transitional words and phrases. Look particularly at the links between paragraphs. Insert transitions to help the reader follow the flow of the text. Such words or phrases as *however, on the one hand/on the other hand, but,* and *in addition* can help the reader see the relationships between ideas.

3 Revising for organization

Once you have decided how to improve the organization of your text, use the CUT, COPY, and PASTE commands to move parts of your text. Rearrange the words, sentences, and paragraphs that comprise your text into the most effective order. Be certain that you check for coherence after rearranging.

4 Revising for development

Your argument is stronger if you include many concrete examples or details. If you are writing an informal piece, do not hesitate to add anecdotes or narratives of personal experiences to give life and personality to your writing. If you are writing a formal paper, you can add information from sources that support your arguments.

5 Revising for tone

In rereading, you may decide that your tone is either too formal or too informal. To revise your tone to be more formal, expand contractions into their full forms, combine some short sentences to make longer sentences, and change informal diction or slang into more formal wording.

6 Revising for format

To convey your information in a more visual way, you may want to add formatting more commonly found in a brochure or a newsletter. You can import and insert graphics to illustrate your text at appropriate points. Try using different fonts by selecting them from the FORMAT menu. Remember, though, that readability of your text is the most important goal; choose fonts accordingly. (See Chapter 7 for more information on fonts.)

7 Writing effective openings, closings, and titles

Openings　Writers have very little time in which to grab the reader's attention—usually only a few seconds. That is why a piece's opening, or lead, is so important. But do not let concern over how you will begin become a stumbling block. Many writers find that leaving the opening for the last stages of revision works best.

Closings or Conclusions   A conclusion usually takes the form of a summary, which points the reader back to the text itself, or speculation, which points the reader outside of the text.

Titles   Because the title is the first thing a reader sees, it must make a good impression. The title also must help the reader anticipate the topic and gain insight into the writer's particular point of view.

1h   Edit

When editing a text, the writer's goal is to make it easier to read. During revision, the writer concentrates on making the piece focused, organized, and well developed. During editing, the writer concentrates on refining words and sentences.

1i   Proofread

Proofreading is the final phase in rewriting. In this stage of the process, writers look closely for distracting punctuation and mechanical errors that will interfere with the reader's understanding. By proofreading after revising and editing, writers can concentrate on details related to manuscript preparation, such as typographical errors, missing words, and irregular spacing, as well as errors in punctuation that they may have missed in earlier stages.

1j   Give and receive feedback

In many writing classes, students work together in peer review groups in which they exchange drafts for review, either electronically via a networked computer system (a local area network, or LAN) or in hard copy form. The instructor also may comment on early drafts and make revision suggestions. Students also may be asked to take their papers to a writing center, where a tutor will read them and offer suggestions. As a writer, you will find it helpful to receive feedback on your work from a variety of sources. Such feedback allows you to become increasingly sensitive to the needs of your readers.

CHAPTER **2**

The Research Project and Using the Internet

The process of writing a research paper does not differ markedly from the process of writing an essay. The difference is one of scope. A research paper is longer than most essays and contains more information from external sources; this information is found by doing research.

WEBLINK

http://www.powa.org

A site devoted to helping writers of research papers

2a Become a researcher

The ability to research—that is, to explore a problem systematically—is a crucial skill for an educated person. A researcher is a careful, critical, systematic thinker who goes beyond memorizing facts on a subject to examine the bases on which claims and arguments rest.

1 Understanding the research project

When you begin a research project, first think through what you will need to do. Ask yourself questions such as

- What will my purpose be?
- How should I sound as a writer?
- Who will my readers be?
- Where will I get my authority?

The two main types of research are primary research and secondary research. Primary research entails generating information or data through processes such as interviewing, administering questionnaires, or observation.

Secondary research involves finding information in secondary, or published, sources. You need to decide which type or types of research your project demands. Discuss with your instructor the kinds of sources that you should be locating and reading for your research project.

2 Selecting a specific topic

Once you have chosen a topic that you are interested in researching, you need to narrow that topic to a specific issue. Preliminary library or Web searches can help you to focus your research.

3 Developing a hypothesis

As you work through the research process, attempting to answer your starting questions, you should come up with a hypothesis—a tentative statement of what you anticipate the research will reveal. A working hypothesis specifically describes a proposition that research evidence will either prove or disprove.

4 Developing a search strategy

A search strategy is a plan for proceeding systematically with research. Once you have decided on your starting questions and working hypothesis, you are ready to outline your search strategy. Your first decision will be about the nature of your research. Will you be relying mostly on secondary (library and Internet) research or on primary (field) research?

The goal of a search is to build a working bibliography—a list of possible sources that may eventually be used in the final paper. A working bibliography is typically about twice as long as the final bibliography for a research paper, because many of the sources you identify will turn out not to be applicable to your paper or not to be available in time for you to use in your research.

2b   Schedule a time frame

If you have never done a research project before, you may be overwhelmed at the thought of such a large and complex task. If you break the job down into smaller parts, however, it will seem much more manageable. It will help to formulate a time frame in which to complete your research project. If your instructor has not given you deadlines, set your own dates for accomplishing specific tasks. Give yourself enough time to plan, organize, and write a first draft and then several revisions.

2c Create a research notebook

It is important to create a notebook in which to record all the information relating to your research project. If you are using a word processor, you can take advantage of its storage capabilities to develop an electronic research notebook. Create a folder, and label it your research notebook. In this folder, you can create files or documents to record your topic and your starting questions, notes from your background research and focused research, and your working bibliography (if you do not have bibliography software).

1 Recording notes in a notebook

Whether the notebook in which you record your notes is handwritten or computer generated, be sure to keep your recorded notes separate from your comments. If your notebook is handwritten, you might use two columns when recording information: one for notes taken from the source and the other for comments, analyses, and queries. If your notebook is electronic, you can use your word-processing program's DOCUMENT COMMENTS feature to INSERT your comments and analyses into the notes taken from sources.

2 Taking notes on note cards

Like notebooks, note cards can be either handwritten or computer generated. If you choose to handwrite notes on index cards, give each note card a descriptive title and take notes on only one side of each card to allow for easy sorting and scanning of information later on. Provide a page reference on your note card for all notes, both quoted and paraphrased. Then consecutively number your notes for each source.

Some computer operating systems and Internet browsers offer computerized note card systems. Such a system can be particularly useful if you own a laptop computer that you can use in the library. You can use the computer note cards just as you would use index cards: title each card by topic, and then type your notes onto the card provided by the computer. The computer note card system will sort the cards automatically by topic.

3 Taking notes with photocopies and printouts

With photocopy machines and computer printers now so readily available in libraries and computer labs, more researchers are making use of these tools to record source information. Making your own photocopies and printouts of sources has many advantages: first, you will have the actual wording of the authors at your fingertips; second, you can highlight passages that are important to your own research for future reference; and third, you can actually take notes on the photocopies or printouts.

When you are researching on the Internet, it might be easiest for you to print out copies of relevant Web pages rather than taking notes by hand. If there is a specific section of a Web page that you wish to use as a source, you can highlight that section using your computer's mouse and then choose PRINT/SELECTION from the PRINT dialog box. In this way, you will print only the parts you need, and not the entire Web site. As with photocopies, printouts of sources from the Internet will also need to have complete bibliographic information.

Another method of obtaining information from the Internet is to download or save Internet pages directly into your own computer files (using FILE>SAVE AS). When downloading or copying and pasting files from the Internet, be especially careful not to import source information directly into your own work without citing the source appropriately. To keep from inadvertently plagiarizing from the Internet, take special care to type into your computer notebook the complete bibliographic information from each source and to put quotation marks around any text that is copied and pasted from the Internet. Also, note for yourself the author of the quotation so that you can use that information in a signal phrase that introduces the quotation.

2d Create a working bibliography

A bibliography is a listing of books and articles on a particular subject. When you submit a research paper, you include a bibliography to show readers what sources you consulted to find your information. As you begin your research, start a working bibliography, which will grow as your research progresses. This working bibliography will likely contain some sources that ultimately you will not use in your research paper, so entries need not be in final bibliographic form. However, it is important to accurately record all the information you will need to compose your final bibliography so that you do not have to track down sources twice.

2e   Gather background information

Now is the time to gather background information, using your starting questions and working hypothesis as a guide. This information will help you conduct more focused research later on.

1 Starting with yourself

At the start of a research project, write down everything you already know about your topic. The list may be quite extensive or rather short. The important thing is to inventory your own knowledge first so that you can systematically build on that knowledge base. The more you know about your topic, the better you will be at judging the value of sources you read. Also, check your biases and assumptions about the topic.

2 Compiling a list of subject headings and keywords

The cataloging system developed by the Library of Congress is the one most widely used for organizing library materials. In order to put information into related categories, the Library of Congress has developed a listing of subject headings. This listing is compiled in a multivolume set called the *Library of Congress Subject Headings* (or *LCSH*), available in both printed and computerized form.

Related to subject headings are keywords (sometimes called descriptors or identifiers), which are used to identify the subjects found in electronic databases, including the Internet. The keywords used to search for electronic sources may not be exactly the same terms that are used by the *LCSH* to categorize the subjects of books and periodicals; each search engine may use its own system of keywords and phrases.

3 Doing preliminary background reading in general reference books

We recommend that you begin your library search in the general reference section. Here you will find reference books that have condensed huge amounts of information into an accessible form. These sources can help you to define your subject area more clearly, to identify keywords and important authors, and to gain a general understanding of your topic. Most reference works are available both in book versions and in computerized versions (either on CDs or on the Internet).

2f Conduct focused research

Once background reading has helped you to understand your subject, narrow it to a manageable size, and formulate a hypothesis, you are ready to read in a more focused way on your topic. Conducting focused secondary research involves locating the specific information you need to write your paper in magazines, newspapers, journals, books, government documents, and the Internet.

1 Using library catalogs

Libraries have catalogs that list all the books and documents they have available. Although some libraries still use card files (which include cards for authors' names, subjects, and book titles), either by themselves or in combination with computerized catalogs, most libraries today house their catalogs on computers. Like card catalogs, most computerized catalogs are searchable by author, title, and subject; in addition, computerized catalogs are searchable by keyword or by a combination of subject and keyword.

2 Using indexes to magazines and newspapers

In your library's general catalog, you'll find a listing of magazine and journal names, but you will not find a listing of specific articles within those publications. Private indexing services such as ERIC (Educational Research Information Clearinghouse) have taken on the job of listing (indexing) all of the individual articles found in specific journals on particular topics; in the case of ERIC, the articles indexed are related to the field of education. To locate articles in education journals on a particular topic, you would use the ERIC descriptors, which are keywords that ERIC uses to index the articles.

3 Using indexes to professional journals

If you are researching a technical or academic subject, you will want to refer to articles written by professionals in the field. Professional journal articles are indexed by indexing services in much the same way as magazine and newspaper articles. However, you will need to find a specialized index or database for professional articles in your particular discipline or subject area. For example, the *Social Sciences Index* lists the titles of articles from journals in the social sciences, and the *General Science Index* lists articles from science journals. Discipline-specific indexes are available in most libraries, both in print and on computer.

4 Using CD-ROMs and other electronic databases

Locating specific information on a topic may require use of a variety of computerized search tools. In addition to your library's computerized catalog and computerized indexes to magazines, newspapers, and journals, investigate any CD-ROM databases available to you. As with any computerized searching, when using CD-ROMs, it is important to know your keywords. Check with the librarian to discern whether there is a thesaurus or listing of subject headings for the particular database you are using. Many libraries subscribe to full-text database services that provide library patrons with Internet access to copies of the actual articles from magazines, newspapers, and professional journals.

5 Using Internet resources

The Internet is becoming an increasingly important research tool in all fields of study. A biologist observed that he can locate information crucial to his research in minutes via the Internet, when it used to take days or even weeks of searching through print sources. See 2g for more on using the Internet for research.

6 Doing primary, or field, research

In all disciplines, researchers use primary research methods to gather information and search for solutions to problems. Primary research methods include *observation, surveys,* and *interviews.*

Observation   The general goal of observation is to describe and perhaps evaluate customary behaviors. Observation is best suited to the collection of nonverbal data. The observer watches people behave in customary ways in a particular environment or setting and takes notes. These "field notes" are used to analyze trends and discern customary behaviors. The disadvantages of observation include lack of control over the environment, lack of quantifiable data, and small sample size.

Surveys   Ideally, an entire population would be studied to gain insights into its society. However, polling an entire population is seldom feasible, so surveys are used to sample small segments of the population selected at random. One common kind of survey is the questionnaire, a form that asks for responses to a set of questions. Designing questions is a science that has been developed over the years. The basic principles are to be sure that the questions you write are clear and understandable and written in such a way that the responses will be easy to tabulate.

Interviews   Interviews are one particular type of survey. The advantages of the interview include flexibility (the questioner can interact with the respondent), speed of response (the questioner immediately knows the responses), and nonverbal behavior (the questioner can gather nonverbal as well as verbal clues).

2g   Use Internet sources throughout the research process

WEBLINK

http://www.lib.berkeley.edu/
TeachingLib/Guides/index
.html

Current information on
Internet searching, from
UC Berkeley librarians

Searching the Internet for information on a topic is similar in many respects to researching in the library. When beginning to research on the Internet, you should follow a search strategy, as outlined in 2a–4. Use the Internet for finding and exploring research topics, for background and focused searching, and even for collaboration with your peers and feedback from your instructor. Email and online discussion forums are ideal ways to try out your topic ideas on your instructor and peers.

2h) Get to know the Internet and the Web

The World Wide Web, a huge spider web-like structure that encompasses computer networks throughout the world, seems to have been woven overnight. But no one spider wove this web; anyone and everyone can contribute (see Chapter 7 for information on designing and writing for the Web). The Web is by far the easiest and most popular way of accessing information from the Internet. The Web provides a hypertext interface for "reading" Internet information. This means that information is presented in the form of a series of links, each leading to another document or another location on the Internet. Documents structured as text with a series of links to other texts are called hypertexts. One simply uses a mouse to click on the link (usually a graphic or a word or phrase in blue type with blue underlining) to connect with the hyperlinked document. Researchers navigate the Web through the use of an Internet browser.

1 Surfing the World Wide Web

You will probably be accessing the Internet through either a direct connection in a campus computer lab or a dial-up modem, cable, or DSL service from home. Direct connections (cable and DSL) are much faster than dial-up modems. If you intend to use your home computer to access the Internet, it is a good idea to check with your campus computing center to find out what they recommend as the best way to connect to the campus computer network.

Once you have an Internet connection, you will need an Internet browser in order for your computer to display Web pages. If you are using a computer in a campus lab, there will probably be icons on the opening screen for the two most popular browsers, *Netscape Communicator* or *Internet Explorer*. They contain comparable features and are free. If you are using a recent version of Windows, you will find that *Internet Explorer* has already been installed on your computer.

2 Keeping track of your search

Both *Netscape* and *Explorer* help you to keep track of important Web sites and to retrace the steps of your Internet search. The GO feature keeps a running list of the Web sites you have visited during your current Internet session. It will disappear when you close down your browser. The GO command is found on the menu bar in *Netscape* and within the VIEW menu in *Explorer*. You can also find the same listing by clicking the arrow to the right of the location box.

If you have found a page that you want to visit frequently, you can add this site's address to your list of bookmarks (*Netscape*) or favorites (*Explorer*). You can add a page to your bookmarks/favorites by visiting that page and then choosing ADD BOOKMARK or ADD TO FAVORITES from the bookmark menu or button.

3 Respecting copyright and avoiding plagiarism

As a student, you need to be careful to behave ethically and responsibly both when using Web materials and when publishing your own work on the Web. In any piece of writing, including Web pages, be certain that you cite all sources, including Internet sources, in a way that readers can locate them easily. Because it is so easy now to simply copy and paste information from the Internet into your own document files, you need to be especially vigilant. See Chapter 3 for more information about using sources responsibly and avoiding plagiarism.

When writing your own Web pages, also be sure to only download images or texts that are considered "freeware," offered by the site to users free of charge. If you are not certain, you should email the author or site sponsor for permission to either download the material or link to it from your own page.

2i ▶ Search the Internet and the Web

Many corporations, nonprofit organizations, and special interest groups maintain information-rich Web sites. The purposes of these sites vary from disseminating information to peddling propaganda to luring customers into spending money. When you use information from an Internet source, remember that unless it is part of a well-known professional organization's site, it probably has not been reviewed by anyone other than members of the organization that maintains the site.

1 Using search tools to locate information

How do you go about finding specific information on a particular topic? The most reliable way is to use one of the Internet search tools. Search tools use different methods of sorting Web pages. Some search tools, often called search engines, use an automated system to sort pages based primarily on the use and placement of keywords. *Altavista* and *Excite* are examples of search engines. Search engines automatically find and catalog new sites as they are added to the Web, indexing information by title and keywords.

2 Searching with keywords

Once you have selected a search engine, you need to determine what search terms to try. Enter a keyword that identifies your topic and search for hits of that keyword—Web pages on which the word appears.

3 Using Boolean operators

One way search tools allow you to focus is by means of Boolean operators, which allow you to expand or limit searches with words such as AND or NOT. Learning to search the Internet and the Web effectively will help you become a better researcher.

CHAPTER **3**

Evaluating and Using Sources: Avoiding Plagiarism

Writers gain credibility through the use of information from experts. It is the responsibility of research authors to be certain that any information from another author, whether paraphrased, summarized, or quoted, is accurately relayed and clearly acknowledged. Integrating source information into one's own writing is a skill that takes practice.

3a Choose legitimate sources

Because you will be relying on your sources to provide the evidence and authority to support your hypothesis, it is crucial that you choose legitimate sources. Your reputation as a researcher may be at stake. Decide whether the source is worth using by considering its relevance; the publisher or sponsor of the source; the author of the material; the timeliness of the piece; and whether this source is cited or cross-referenced in any other works.

For a Web site, look at the domain type to find out some information about the sponsor of the site. Common domain types include

- Education (.edu)
- Government (.gov)
- Nonprofit organization (.org)
- Commercial (.com)
- Network (.net)
- Military (.mil)
- Other countries (.ca for Canada; .uk for United Kingdom)

Being careless about your sources can lead to a serious academic offense called plagiarism—with serious consequences such as a failing grade for the course or even expulsion from school. **Plagiarism** is defined as the unauthorized or misleading use of the language and text of another author. Whenever you use exact words from a source, this must be indicated clearly through the use of a signal phrase, quotation marks, and an in-text citation at the point in the text where the source information is quoted. Readers must be able to tell as they are reading your paper exactly what information came from which source and what information is your own contribution to the paper. (See 3c.)

3b Use sources responsibly

WEBLINK

http://www.wisc.edu/writing/Handbook/QPA_add.html

Detailed explanations and examples of using quotations, paraphrases, and summaries

When writing a research paper, you must acknowledge any original information, ideas, and illustrations that you find in another author's work, whether it is in print or on the Internet. Acknowledging the work of other authors is called documenting sources. (The appropriate forms for documentation are discussed in Chapters 5 and 6.)

3c   Avoid plagiarism

If you use source information carefully and accurately, you will avoid any charges of plagiarism. By following the guidelines in this chapter when you paraphrase, summarize, and quote, you will never plagiarize.

Acknowledgment Required   Any word, phrase, or sentence that you copied directly from a source must be placed in quotation marks, and complete bibliographic information must be given, including the page reference for the quotation. Similarly, you must acknowledge paraphrases and summary restatements of ideas taken from a source, even though you have cast them in your own words.

No Acknowledgment Required   You need not document "common knowledge." This term refers to information that is generally known or accepted by educated people. Information that you can find readily in general reference works such as encyclopedias or in the popular media is probably common knowledge and need not be documented, although it must be stated in your own words. Well-proven historical facts and dates need not be documented.

Unintentional Plagiarism   Your notes should accurately record source information in your own words. You should be able to tell at a glance from your notes when information is from a source and when it is your own commentary or thoughts on a source. Students taking notes from a source sometimes commit *unintentional* plagiarism by carelessly copying words and phrases from a source into their notes and then using these words and phrases without acknowledgment in a paper.

Intentional Plagiarism   Sometimes plagiarism is *intentional*; that is, a writer knowingly copies the work of another without proper acknowledgment of the source. Whenever you use words from a source, this must be indicated clearly through the use of quotation marks and documentation at the point in the text where the source information is used. It is not enough to list the author in the footnotes or bibliography. Readers must be able to tell as they are reading your paper exactly what information came from which source and what information is your contribution to the paper. That way, they can follow your research trail and form their own judgments.

3d   Paraphrase sources accurately

Instead of directly quoting from sources, writers have the option of *paraphrasing* source information. The objective of paraphrasing is to present an author's ideas clearly, using your own words and phrases instead of those of the author. This important skill not only deepens your understanding of the author's ideas but also helps you to avoid plagiarism.

With paraphrases, as with quotations, you must indicate exactly on what page in the source you found the information. Ideally, anyone else reading your work should be able to locate the exact wording from which your paraphrase was taken.

3e   Summarize sources briefly

Summaries condense the information found in sources. Like paraphrasing, summarizing involves restating the author's ideas or information in your own words, but summaries are typically much briefer than the original information. The goal of a summary is to record the gist of the piece—its primary line of argument—without tangential arguments, examples, and other departures from the main ideas. As with paraphrasing, you need to be sure that the summary is stated in your own words.

1 Recording summaries in notes

When you first preview a source to determine its relevance to your research, you can also decide how much of the source you are likely to use in your paper. You would not want to paraphrase an entire article, for example, if only the introduction related to your topic. Rather, you could simply summarize the relevant portion.

2 Integrating summaries into a paper

Summaries are incorporated into a paper in much the same way as direct quotations and paraphrases. Introduce a summary with a signal phrase, place it in a context for the readers, or perhaps use the author's name or article title in the introduction. As with quoting and paraphrasing, you need to provide documentation indicating the source of the summarized information.

3 Avoiding plagiarism when summarizing

Using your own words and providing documentation for the source will produce a summary that avoids plagiarism. A summary that uses the same wording and sentence structure of the original source and that fails to provide documentation may be plagiarism.

3f   Quote sources sparingly

Quotations are exact wordings taken from sources. Use direct quotations sparingly in a research paper. A string of quotations can be confusing for readers, especially if each presents information in a different writing style. By paraphrasing and summarizing instead of quoting, you can more smoothly incorporate the ideas from sources into your own writing. However, if an author uses unique language or an interesting image, a brief quotation may be an effective addition to a paper.

1 Using quoted material

When you quote from a source, it is important to be accurate. Making photocopies or printouts of a source can help you to quote exactly because you can recheck the wording from the original. Every time you copy information from a source, indicate through quotation marks on your note card that you have taken the exact wording from the original.

2 Integrating quotations into a paper

When you use a direct quotation, you must integrate it smoothly into the flow of your ideas. Use signal phrases to alert your reader that a quotation is coming. Make sure to attribute the source appropriately (see Chapters 5 and 6 on documentation formats) and punctuate it correctly (see Chapter 20 on Quotation Marks). The quotations that you use should be relatively short to minimize interruption.

CHAPTER **4**

Writing the Research Paper

Now that you have gathered and evaluated your information, you need to step back and assess just where all this research has taken you. Although the writing process that you will follow in writing your research paper is not radically different from the writing process outlined earlier in this handbook, there are some important differences. The first difference is one of scope; a research paper is longer than most essays. Sometimes students find themselves overwhelmed by the sheer volume of information they have collected. It is indeed a huge challenge to organize and present research.

4a Review your purpose, audience, and thesis

Remind yourself of your intended purpose for writing the research paper. Ask yourself, "Who is my audience?" You may not be able to determine for certain who your readers will be, but you can assume that they will be intelligent people who have an interest in the topic you are writing about. It is unlikely that they will be experts in the field you are discussing; therefore, you should define any terms carefully and avoid using jargon or technical vocabulary.

1 Writing a thesis statement

A thesis statement for a research paper is similar to a thesis statement for an essay. That is, it states for readers the central idea that the paper will argue. Many times, the working thesis statement is revised during the actual writing process.

2 Revising the thesis

Most research papers argue a position. However, some research papers are informational; that is, they report on information without taking a position.

Your teacher may require that your thesis (and thus your research paper) have an argumentative edge. If so, make sure that you have taken a stand that can be supported through arguments in the paper.

3 Deciding on a voice and tone

Academic papers should be informative and serious, but they need not be dull or dry. You can still put your own personality into a piece. Although it is generally not appropriate to adopt too informal a tone for an academic research paper, taking yourself out of the piece entirely may leave readers with the impression that the piece is lifeless and uninteresting. Try to strike a balance in your tone, making it pleasing to readers.

4b   Plan a structure

Some writers like to work from an organizational plan or outline, fleshing out the skeleton by incorporating additional information under each of the major points and subpoints. Others prefer to begin writing and have the structure evolve more organically. You need not be overly concerned about formal structure at this point, unless your teacher stipulates a particular outline format.

4c   Write a draft

Now you should be ready to begin drafting your research paper. Remind yourself of your general understanding of the topic, of your starting questions and hypothesis, and of the answers to the questions as stated in your thesis. When writing your first draft, use concrete and simple language to explain in your own words your research conclusions. Ideally, you should type your draft on a computer to make revisions easier.

1 Choosing a drafting strategy

You will need to establish your own strategy for writing a first draft, one that fits your writing style. Here are a few different ways in which writers of research projects proceed:

- Write a draft systematically from a plan, using the building-block technique (see 1e-1).
- Write a draft using the top-down method (see 1e-2).
- Write a rough first draft and then write a revision outline that suggests ways in which the draft needs to be changed.
- Write a draft using your handwritten or electronic note cards (see 2c-2), or your photocopied or printed-out sources (see 2c-3).

2 Applying the drafting strategy to blend material

As you draft, you blend your own knowledge and material from sources. In writing a first draft, it is best to put down your own understanding of the topic first, rather than relying too heavily on your sources. After you have written your draft, you can go back and add specific sources to support your arguments. Readers want to know what *you* think about the subject. They do not want to read a string of quotations loosely joined by transitions.

3 Writing an introduction and conclusion

Composing introductions and conclusions is discussed in 1g-7. Because a research paper typically covers more information than an essay, it may take a couple of paragraphs to introduce the topic effectively. You should make certain that both your introduction and your conclusion help readers to understand your research paper's main point.

4d Review and revise the draft

A great deal of important work remains to be done on your paper once you complete a rough draft. You must revise the paper to make the most effective possible presentation of the research. Readers expect you to be clear and correct; they should not be distracted by ambiguous source references, confusing language, or incorrect punctuation. It is a good idea to set your draft aside for a day or two, if time allows, so that you can look at it with a fresh eye. It is also a good idea to gather as much feedback as you can from peers. Plan to exchange drafts with a classmate or two for their suggestions (see 1j for more on giving and receiving feedback).

4e Follow formatting conventions

Research paper formatting conventions are those customary ways of presenting information that have developed in various disciplines. Ask your instructor if there is a particular format you should use. If not, select the format from the discipline most closely related to your research topic. Documentation formats for different disciplines are provided in Chapters 5 and 6.

PART 2 Documentation

CHAPTER 5

MLA Documentation

The Modern Language Association (MLA) system of documentation has been adopted by many scholarly writers in the fields of language and literature (Joseph Gibaldi, *MLA Handbook for Writers of Research Papers,* 6th ed., New York: MLA, 2003). The MLA system consists of in-text citations (found in parentheses) and an alphabetical listing of works cited (found at the end of the paper). For humanities researchers, specific sources and the pages on which information can be found are more important than the date on which the source was published. Thus, in-text citations in the MLA system include the author's last name and the page number of the source information.

A Directory to the MLA System

In-Text Citations

(Continued)

In-Text Citations *(Continued)*

Works Cited Entries

Books

(Continued)

Works Cited Entries *(Continued)*

(Continued)

5a Integrate sources and avoid plagiarism in the MLA system

In Chapter 3 "Evaluating and Using Sources: Avoiding Plagiarism," we talked in general about the importance of using sources accurately and responsibly in your research papers. To help you do so, the MLA citation format provides for a two-part system of source identification: (1) parenthetical references within the body of the paper (discussed in 5b), and (2) a Works Cited list at the end of the paper (discussed in 5d). By using the MLA system, you can integrate your source information appropriately and ethically without inadvertently committing plagiarism.

The MLA Citation System

1. Introduce your source using a *signal phrase* that names its author: According to Jones, . . .
2. Paraphrase or summarize the information from your source. It's best to use direct quotations sparingly. Rather, recast the source information into your own words. If you do use any words or phrases from the author, however, be sure to include them in quotation marks.
3. At the conclusion of your paraphrase, summary, or quotation, insert in parentheses the page number on which the information was found, followed by a period: (332).
4. At the end of your paper, list the source with complete bibliographic information on your Works Cited page.

Plagiarism, a serious academic offense, is often committed by students inadvertently in the following two ways:

1. Failing to acknowledge a summary or paraphrase of a source in the body of the paper through a signal phrase and parenthetical citation.
2. Using the original authors' words without putting the borrowed words or phrases in quotation marks or including a parenthetical citation.

1 Acknowledge all sources

A successful research paper will be written as an argument in the writer's own words, expressing an understanding of the answers to specific research questions. In such a paper, sources are used as evidence in support of the writer's argument. Source support is integrated into the flow of the research paper through the use of paraphrases and summaries in the writer's own words; each source is acknowledged by a parenthetical citation. Failing to acknowledge a source results in plagiarism. In addition to paraphrases and summaries, any other source material must also be acknowledged, such as specific facts, graphics or visuals, cartoons, diagrams, or charts, using the two-part MLA citation system.

2 Indicate original source words and phrases with quotation marks

The best research papers use direct quotations sparingly as support for their own ideas and integrate those quotations smoothly into the flow of the paper. A signal phrase alerts the reader that a direct quotation follows; the quotation marks show exactly which words and phrases are being quoted. Long quotations are formatted using indentation rather than quotation marks. Carelessness at the note-taking stage can result in unintentional plagiarism (see 3c).

5b Use the MLA system for in-text citations

In the MLA documentation system, citations within the body of the paper are linked to the Works Cited list at the end. The in-text citations are sometimes called *parenthetical references*, because the documentation is placed within parentheses. Both the author who is being cited and the page number of the source (when known) are included in the in-text citation in the MLA system. Following are some guidelines for incorporating parenthetical citations in the text of your research paper.

1. Author Named in the Narrative

If a paraphrase or direct quotation is introduced with the name of the author in a signal phrase, simply indicate the page number of the source in parentheses at the end of the cited material.

Attempting to define ethnic stereotyping, Gordon Allport states that

"much prejudice is a matter of blind conformity with prevailing folkways"

(12).

No page number is necessary when an entire work is cited. (Note that titles of independently published works are underlined.)

Conrad's book Lord Jim tells the story of an idealistic young Englishman.

2. *Author Not Named in the Narrative*

If the author's name is not used to introduce the paraphrased or quoted material, place the author's last name along with the specific page number in parentheses at the end of the cited material. Do not separate author and page number with a comma. Note that the parenthetical material precedes the sentence's end punctuation.

```
When Mitford and Peter Rodd were first engaged, "they even bought black
shirts and went to some Fascist meetings" (Guinness 304).
```

3. *Multiple Sentences Paraphrased*

Indicate every instance of paraphrased or summarized material. If an entire paragraph is paraphrased from a single source, mention the author's name at the beginning of the paragraph and cite the page number where appropriate.

```
    As Endelman shows, the turbulence of the interwar years--"political
agitation, social discrimination, street hooliganism" (191)--culminated
in the formation of the British Union of Fascists. He states that anti-
Semitism "was common enough that few Jews could have avoided it
altogether or been unaware of its existence" (194).
```

4. *Work by Two or Three Authors*

Include the last names of all the authors (the last two connected by *and*) either in the text or in the parenthetical reference. Because the following reference is to the entire work, no page number is necessary.

```
Goodsell, Maher, and Tinto write about how the theory of collaborative
learning may be applied to the administration of a college or university.
```

5. *Work by Four or More Authors*

In citing a work by four or more authors, either provide the last names of all the authors or provide the name of the first author followed by the abbreviation *et al.* ("and others").

In The Development of Writing Abilities, the authors present a theory of
writing based upon whether a writer assumes a participant or a spectator
role (Britton et al.).

6. Work by a Corporate Author

When the author is an organization or corporation, treat the group's
name the same way as the name of an individual author. If the name is long,
try to incorporate it into the text rather than including it in a parenthetical
note.

The book The Downsizing of America, by the New York Times, quotes a
report as showing "that 131,209 workers had been cast out of their jobs
in just the first quarter of 1996" (220).

7. Work in More than One Volume

If the work consists of more than one volume, provide the volume number, followed by a colon, just before the page number.

In Ward's introduction to the collected works of Sir John Vanbrugh, he
states that "the Vanbrugh family seems to have been both ancient and
honorable" (1:x).

When referring to an entire volume of a multivolume work, add a
comma after the author's name, followed by *vol.* and the volume number.

8. Different Works by the Same Author

When the Works Cited list refers to two works by the same author, include in the parenthetical reference the title (which may be abbreviated), as
well as the author and the page number of the source. If the author's name is
included in the text, cite only the title and page number in parentheses.

Her first volume of memoirs, published in 1975, tells the story of her
brother's friend (Mitchison, All Change Here 85). In her pre-war novel,
Mitchison, who was the housebound wife of an Oxford don, derives a

```
strange solution to England's economic problems (We Have Been Warned
```
```
441).
```

9. Two or More Authors with the Same Last Name

Include both the authors' first and last names in the signal phrase or in parentheses to distinguish two authors who have the same last name.

```
Luci Shaw reveals deep spirituality in her poem entitled "Made flesh"
```
```
(31).
```

10. Work Cited Indirectly

If possible, take information directly from the original source. However, sometimes it is necessary to cite someone indirectly—particularly in the case of a published account of someone's spoken words. To indicate an indirect quotation, use the abbreviation *qtd. in* (for "quoted in") before listing the source.

```
High school teacher Ruth Gerrard finds that "certain Shakespearean
```
```
characters have definite potential as student role models" (qtd. in Davis
```
```
and Salomone 24).
```

11. Two or More Sources within the Same Citation

When referring to two or more sources within the same parenthetical reference, use semicolons to separate the citations. For the sake of readability, however, take care not to list too many sources in a single citation.

```
The works of several authors in the post-war years tend to focus on
```
```
racial themes (Mitchison 440; Mosley 198).
```

12. Anonymous Work

Sources such as magazine articles, Web sites, and reports by commissions may not list an author. Such works are listed by their title on the Works Cited page. For the in-text citation of an anonymous work listed by title, use an abbreviated version of the title, in parentheses.

The article points out the miscommunications that can occur between men
and women because of differences in communication styles ("It Started").

13. *Work of Literature*

Classic works of literature are often available in different editions. It is
therefore helpful to include location information, such as chapter number,
section number, or act and scene number, in the parenthetical reference so that
the reader can locate the reference in any edition of the work. Include this location information after a page reference, where appropriate. When citing
classic poetry or plays, use the line numbers instead of page numbers.
Generally, use arabic numbers rather than roman numerals.

In the novel <u>Lord Jim</u>, Conrad describes the village of Patusan and its
inhabitants (242; ch. 24).

In <u>Paradise Lost</u>, Satan's descent to earth is described in graphic detail
(Milton 4.9-31).

As Laertes leaves for France, Polonius gives the young man trite and
unhelpful advice such as "Beware / Of entrance to a quarrel; but being
in / Bear't that th' opposed may beware of thee" (<u>Hamlet</u> 1.3.65-67).

14. *Work in an Anthology*

If you are citing a work found in an anthology (collection), use the name
of the author of the particular work you are citing, not the editor(s) of the anthology. List the page numbers as they are found in the anthology.

The American Dream crosses many ethnic boundaries, as illustrated by
Papaleo (88).

15. *Bible*

When quoting from the Bible, give the title of the version (e.g., *The
Revised Standard Version*), the book of the Bible, the chapter and verse (separated by a period). If using a signal phrase, spell out the book of the Bible

being quoted. In parentheses, abbreviate the book of the Bible if its name is five or more letters (e.g., Phil. for Philippians).

In his letter to the Philippians, the apostle Paul says, "There must be no room for rivalry and personal vanity among you, but you must humbly reckon others better than yourselves. Look to each other's interest and not merely to your own" (The New English Bible, Phil. 2.3-4).

16. *Entire Work or One Page Article*

When citing an entire work or a work that is only one page long, refer to the text in a signal phrase by the author and title without any page numbers.

In his book Losing My Mind: An Intimate Look at Life with Alzheimer's, Thomas DeBaggio chronicles his battle with Alzheimer's disease.

17. *Work with No Page Numbers*

If you are citing a work that does not have any page numbers listed, you may omit the page number from your citation. If a work uses paragraph numbers instead of page numbers, use the abbreviation *par(s)*.

The reporter from a recent Family Law Conference sponsored by the American Bar Association, Sarah H. Ramsey, stated, "High-conflict custody cases are marked by a lack of trust between the parents, a high level of anger and a willingness to engage in repetitive litigation" (par. 24).

18. *Electronic Source or Web Site*

When information is from an electronic medium, usually the entire work is referenced. In such cases, incorporate the reference to the work within the sentence by naming the author of the source (or the title, if no author is listed) just as it is listed on the Works Cited page.

One of the features of The Encyclopedia Mythica Web site is its archive of cultural myths, such as those prevalent in Native-American society.

When citing a Web site with secondary pages, list separately each secondary page used in the research paper. Be sure that the Works Cited list includes the correct URL for each secondary page and lists each page independently by its title.

According to Britannica Online, in Native-American mythology, a feather

often symbolizes a prayer ("Feather").

When quoting or paraphrasing directly from an electronic source, either give the section title in quotation marks (as in the example above) or cite the paragraph number (with the abbreviation *par.*), if provided, so that a reader will be able to find the section used in the paper. If no numbering is provided, list the source author or title only.

The writer discusses his reasons for calling Xerox's online site "a great

place to visit" (Gomes, par. 5).

The average global air temperature has risen between 0.3 and 0.6 degree

Celsius (Hileman).

5c Format bibliographic footnotes according to the MLA system

Generally, footnotes and endnotes are not used in the MLA system of documentation. However, notes may be included to refer the reader to sources that contain information different from the content of the paper. In the text, indicate a note with a superscript number typed immediately after the source that is referred to. Number notes consecutively throughout the text.

Use a note to cite sources that have additional information on topics covered in the paper.

[1]For further information on this point, see Barbera (168), McBrien

(56), and Kristeva (29).

Use a note to cite sources that contain information related to that included in the paper.

²Although outside the scope of this paper, major themes in the novel are discussed by Kristeva and Barbera.

Use a note to cite sources containing information that a reader might want to compare with that in the paper.

³On this point, see also Rosenblatt's <u>Literature as Exploration</u>, in which she discusses reader response theory.

For the endnote format, start a new page following the end of the text, before the Works Cited list. Type the title "Notes," centered horizontally one inch from the top of the page. Double-space to the first note. Indent the first line five spaces (or ½ inch) from the left margin, and type the note number slightly above the line (or use the superscript format on a word processor). Follow this number with one space and then the text of the note. Double-space between and within all notes.

For the footnote format, position the text of the note at the bottom of the page on which the reference occurs. Begin the footnote four lines below the text. Single-space within a footnote, but double-space between footnotes if more than one note appears on a page. On the Works Cited page, include all the sources mentioned in the notes.

5d Format the Works Cited page according to the MLA system

The alphabetical listing of all the sources used in a paper, usually entitled Works Cited, comes at the end of the paper. Other names for this listing include Bibliography, Literature Cited, Works Consulted (which includes works not directly cited), and Annotated Bibliography (which includes brief summaries of sources). Check with your instructor to determine which format she or he prefers. The purpose of this listing is to help readers find the information used in the paper, so the entries must be complete and accurate.

List sources alphabetically by the last name of the author, using the letter-by-letter system of alphabetization. When no author is given, alphabetize by the first word of the title (excluding *A, An,* or *The*). Type the first word of each entry at the left margin. Indent subsequent lines of the same entry five spaces (or $\frac{1}{2}$ inch). Double-space the entire reference page, both between and within entries.

When you have more than one work by the same author, arrange the titles alphabetically. Give the author's name for the first entry only. For subsequent works by the same author, substitute three hyphens (followed by a period) for the author's name.

Books   A citation for a book has three basic parts:

Author's Name. <u>Book Title</u>. Publication Information.

For books, monographs, and other complete works, include the author's full name as given on the title page—start with the last name first, followed by a comma; then put the first name and middle name or initial followed by a period. After the author's name, give the complete title of the work as it appears on the title page (underlined), followed by a period. Important words in the title should be capitalized. Include the subtitle, if there is one, separated from the title by a colon. Next, include (if appropriate) the name of the editor, compiler, or translator; the edition of the book; the number of volumes; and the name of the series. Finally, indicate the place of publication, followed by a colon (if several cities are listed, include only the first one); the publisher's name as it appears on the title page, followed by a comma; and the date of publication from the copyright page, followed by a period.

In MLA style, the publication information is abbreviated as much as is possible in the bibliographic entry. The city where the book was published is given without a state abbreviation, unless the city may be unfamiliar (*Redmond, WA*) or confused with another city (*Springfield, MA*). A country abbreviation may be needed for clarity for some foreign publications (for example, *Ulster, Ire.; Bergen, Norw.*). But if a foreign city is well known (such as London or Paris), a country abbreviation is unnecessary. Shorten the publisher's name to one word wherever possible (for example, McGraw-Hill, Inc. to *McGraw*; Houghton Mifflin Co. to *Houghton*). Similarly, abbreviate the names of university and government presses: *Columbia UP* stands for Columbia University Press; the letters *GPO* for Government Printing Office. (For guidelines on citing electronic books, see page 57.)

Note: Unless your instructor directs you differently, show the title of a complete work or a journal in underlined form, even though such titles appear in italics in most printed documents.

1. Book by One Author

Author's Name	Book Title	Publication Information

Allport, Gordon W. <u>The Nature of Prejudice</u>. Palo Alto: Addison, 1954.

Haire-Sargeant, Lin. <u>H</u>. New York: Pocket, 1992.

Manguel, Alberto. <u>A History of Reading</u>. New York: Viking, 1996.

2. Book by Two or Three Authors

Write multiple authors' names in the order in which they are given on the book's title page. Note that this order may not be alphabetical. Reverse the name of the first author only, putting the last name first; separate the authors' names with commas.

Goodsell, Anne S., Michelle R. Maher, and Vincent Tinto. <u>Collaborative</u>

<u>Learning: A Sourcebook for Higher Education</u>. University Park:

National Center on Postsecondary Teaching, Learning, and Assessment,

1992.

3. Book by More than Three Authors

For a book with more than three authors, either write out the names of all the authors listed on the book's title page or write only the first author's name, followed by a comma and the Latin phrase *et al.* (for "and others").

Britton, James, Tony Burgess, Nancy Martin, Alex McLeod, and Harold Rosen.

<u>The Development of Writing Abilities</u>. London: Macmillan, 1975.

Britton, James, et al. <u>The Development of Writing Abilities</u>. London:

Macmillan, 1975.

4. Organization as Author

When an organization rather than an individual is the author, give the name of the organization as listed on the title page instead of the author, even if the same group also published the book.

Alzheimer's Disease and Related Disorders Association. <u>Understanding</u>

<u>Alzheimer's Disease</u>. New York: Scribner's, 1988.

5. *Book by a Corporate Author*

A book by a corporate author is any book whose title page lists as the author a group, rather than individuals. Start with the name of the corporate author, even if it is also the publisher.

Conference on College Composition and Communication. <u>The National</u>

<u>Language Policy</u>. Urbana: NCTE, 1992.

6. *Unknown Author*

If no author is listed, begin the entry with the title. List the work on your references listing alphabetically by the first major word in the title instead of by the author.

<u>The American Heritage Dictionary of the English Language</u>. 3rd ed. Boston:

Houghton, 1996.

7. *Book with an Editor*

For books with editors rather than authors, start with the editor or editors, followed by a comma and the abbreviation *ed.* (for "editor") or *eds.* (for "editors").

Barbera, Jack, and William McBrien, eds. <u>Me Again: The Uncollected</u>

<u>Writings of Stevie Smith</u>. New York: Farrar, 1982.

8. *Chapter or Selection from an Edited Work*

An entry for a particular selection needs to begin with the author's name and the title of the selection. The title is underlined if the work is a book or a play; it is enclosed in quotation marks if the work is a poem, short story, chapter, or essay. Note that the name of the editor or editors follows the book title and is preceded by the abbreviation *Ed.* (for "Edited by"). The inclusive page numbers of the work follow the publication information.

Bambara, Toni Cade. "Raymond's Run." <u>The Norton Anthology of African</u>

<u>American Literature</u>. Ed. Henry Louis Gates, Jr., and Nellie Y.

McKay. New York: Norton, 1997. 2307-13.

9. Book with Author and Editor

When citing the book itself, begin with the author's name, followed by the editor's name, introduced by *Ed.* after the title.

L'Engle, Madeleine. O Sapientia. Ed. Luci Shaw. Wheaton, IL: Harold Shaw,

1984.

When citing the editor's contribution to the work, begin with the editor's name followed by a comma and *ed.* Then list the author's name, introduced by *By*, following the title.

Shaw, Luci, ed. O Sapientia. By Madeleine L'Engle. Wheaton, IL: Harold

Shaw, 1984.

10. Two or More Items from an Anthology

When citing more than one work from an anthology, list the anthology itself in your Works Cited.

Madison, Soyini D., ed. The Woman That I Am: The Literature and Culture

of Contemporary Women of Color. New York: St. Martin's, 1994.

11. Two or More Books by the Same Author

Alphabetize entries by the first word in the title. Include the author's name in the first entry only. In subsequent entries, type three hyphens in place of the author's name, followed by a period.

Rose, Mike. Lives on the Boundary: A Moving Account of the Struggles and

Achievements of America's Educationally Underprepared. New York:

Penguin, 1989.

---.Possible Lives: The Promise of Education in America. Boston:

Houghton, 1995.

12. Article in a Reference Book

An entry for an article in a reference book follows the same pattern as an entry for a work in an anthology. Note, however, that the editor's name and full publication information need not be provided; it is sufficient to provide the edition (if known) and the year of publication. If the article is signed, provide the author's name. (Often the author's name is given in abbreviated form at the end of the article and included in full form elsewhere.)

Robins, Robert Henry. "Language." Encyclopaedia Britannica. 1980 ed.

If the article is unsigned, start with the title of the article:

"Lochinvar." Merriam-Webster's Encyclopedia of Literature. 1995 ed.

13. Introduction, Preface, Foreword, or Afterword

Start with the name of the author of the specific part being cited, followed by the name of the part, capitalized but not underlined or enclosed in quotation marks. If the writer of the specific part is the same as the author of the book, give the author's last name, preceded by the word *By*. If the writer of the specific part is different from the author of the book, give the book author's complete name after *By*. Provide complete publication information and inclusive page numbers (even if they are given as Roman numerals) of the part being cited.

Tompkins, Jame. Preface. A Life in School: What the Teacher Learned. By

　　Tompkins. Reading: Addison, 1996. xi-xix.

14. Book in Translation

Begin the entry with the author's name and the title of the book. After the book's title, insert the abbreviation *Trans.* (for "Translated by") and give the translator's name. If the book also has an editor, give the names of the editor and the translator in the order in which they are listed on the title page.

Kristeva, Julia. Powers of Horror: An Essay on Abjection. Trans. Leon S.

　　Roudiez. New York: Columbia UP, 1982.

15. Second or Subsequent Edition of a Book

If a book is not a first edition, identify the edition in the way that it is identified on the book's title page: by year (*1993 ed.*), by name (*Rev. ed.* for "Revised edition"), or by number (*2nd ed., 3rd ed.*).

White, Edward M. Teaching and Assessing Writing. 2nd ed. San Francisco:

　　Jossey-Bass, 1994.

16. Work in More than One Volume

When citing more than one volume of a multivolume work, insert the total number of volumes in the work before the publication material.

Doyle, Arthur Conan. <u>The Complete Sherlock Holmes</u>. 2 vols. Garden City:

    Doubleday. 1930.

17. One Volume of a Multivolume Work

Provide the author and title followed by the volume number of the volume you are citing. At the end of the citation, following the date, provide the number of volumes in the complete work.

Poe, Edgar Allan. <u>The Complete Poems and Stories of Edgar Allan Poe</u>. Vol

    1. New York: Knopf, 1982. 2 vols.

18. Book in a Series

If the title page indicates that the book is part of a series, insert the series name (do not underline it or enclose it in quotation marks) and the series number, if any, before the publication material.

Berlin, James A. <u>Rhetorics, Poetics, and Cultures</u>. Refiguring College

    English Studies. Urbana: NCTE, 1996.

19. Republished Book

Insert the original publication date, followed by a period, before the publication material of the work being cited.

Dewey, John. <u>Experience and Education</u>. 1938. New York: Collier, 1963.

20. Government Document

If the author of a government document is unknown, start with the name of the government, followed by the name of the agency that issued the document, abbreviated. The title of the publication, underlined, follows, and the usual publication material completes the entry.

United States. FBI. <u>Uniform Crime Reports for the United States: 1995</u>.

    Washington: GPO, 1995.

(*GPO* stands for Government Printing Office.)

21. *Published Proceedings of a Conference*

Write an entry for proceedings in the same way as for a book. Provide information about the conference after the title of the proceedings.

Kelder, Richard, ed. <u>Interdisciplinary Curricula, General Education, and Liberal Learning</u>. Selected Papers from the Third Annual Conference of the Institute for the Study of Postsecondary Pedagogy, Oct. 1992. New Paltz: SUNY New Paltz, 1993.

22. *Pamphlet or Newsletter*

Cite a pamphlet the same way that you would cite a book.

<u>Presbyterian Peacemaking Program</u>. Peacemaking Pamphlets. Louisville: Presbyterian Church USA, 1996.

23. *Title within Another Title*

If there is a title of another book within the title of the book you are citing, do not underline that title within another title.

Steinbeck, John. <u>Journal of a Novel</u>: The East of Eden <u>Letters</u>. New York: Viking, 1969.

24. *Sacred Book*

When citing an individual published edition of a sacred book, begin the entry with the title, including the specific version.

<u>The Torah: The Five Books of Moses</u>. Philadelphia: The Jewish Society of America, 1962.

Periodicals A citation for an article in a periodical follows a format similar to that for a book:

Author's Name. "Title of the Article." Publication Information.

In the publication information, the title of the journal, as it appears on the journal's title page (without introductory articles such as *A* and *The*), is underlined. The volume and issue numbers, if provided, go after the journal title and are followed by the publication date, in parentheses. A colon follows the parentheses. Then, inclusive page numbers are provided for the entire article.

When citing magazines and newspapers, list the day and month (abbreviated except for May, June, and July) of publication, with the day before the month, followed by the year (*19 Dec. 1997*). Provide page numbers for the entire article. Note that if the article is not printed on consecutive pages, you need to provide only the first page number and a plus sign, with no space between them. (For guidelines on citing articles in online periodicals, see page 58.)

25. Article in a Journal Paginated by Volume

Many professional journals are numbered continuously, from the first page of the first issue to the final page of the last issue within a volume. Do not include an issue number when citing this kind of journal.

```
        Author                    Article Title
┌─────────────┐ ┌───────────────────────────────────┐
Bloom, Lynn Z. "Why I (Used to) Hate to Give Grades."

    College Composition and Communication 48 (1997): 360-71.
    └────────────────────────────────────┘ └┘ └──────┘ └─────────┘
                Journal Title              Volume/ Year of  Consecutive
                                           Number Publication  Pages
```

When there are two or more authors, write the authors' names in the order in which they are given on the first page of the article. Note that this order may not be alphabetical. Reverse the name of the first author only (putting the last name first).

Kidda, Michael, Joseph Turner, and Frank E. Parker. "There Is an

   Alternative to Remedial Education." Metropolitan Universities 3

   (1993): 16-25.

26. Article in a Journal Paginated by Issue

If each issue of the journal is numbered separately, starting with page 1, include both volume and issue numbers. Put a period after the volume number, and write the issue number after the period—for example, 12.1 signifies volume 12, issue 1.

Mohanty, S. P. "Us and Them: On the Philosophical Bases of Political

    Criticism." <u>Yale Journal of Criticism</u> 2.2 (1989): 1-31.

27. *Magazine Article*

If the article is unsigned, begin with the title. For a weekly or biweekly magazine, provide the day, the month (abbreviated, except for May, June, and July), and the year, followed by a colon and the inclusive page numbers.

"It Started in a Garden." <u>Time</u> 22 Sept. 1952: 110-11.

For a monthly or quarterly magazine, give only the month or quarter and the year before the inclusive page numbers. (If the article is not printed on consecutive pages, give the first page number followed by a plus sign.)

MacDonald, Heather. "Downward Mobility: The Failure of Open Admissions at

    City University." <u>City Journal</u> Summer 1994: 10-20.

28. *Newspaper Article*

Provide the name of the newspaper, but do not use the article (*The, An, A*) that precedes it (*Boston Globe,* not *The Boston Globe*). If it is not included in the newspaper's title, add the city of publication in brackets following the title. Nationally published newspapers, such as *USA Today*, do not need a city of publication in the reference. Next, provide the day, month (abbreviated, except for May, June, and July), and year. (Do not list volume or issue numbers; however, if the edition is given on the newspaper's masthead, do include it, followed by a colon.) Conclude the entry by providing the page numbers, preceded by the section number or letter if each section is separately paginated.

Doherty, William F. "Woodward Jury Seeks Definitions." <u>Boston Globe</u> 29

    Oct. 1997: B1+.

"Twenty Percent Biased Against Jews." <u>New York Times</u> 22 Nov. 1992: A1.

29. *Editorial*

Provide the name of the editorial writer (last name first), if known, and then the title of the editorial (in quotation marks). Next, write the word *Editorial*, but do not underline it or enclose it is quotation marks. End the entry with the name of the newspaper, magazine, or journal and the standard publication information.

Paglia, Carnille. "More Mush from the NEA." Editorial. <u>Wall Street</u>

    <u>Journal</u> 24 Oct. 1997: A22.

30. Letter to the Editor

Include the designation *Letter* after the name of the letter writer, but do not underline it or enclose it in quotation marks. End the entry with the name of the newspaper, magazine, or journal and the standard publication information.

Schack, Steven. Letter. <u>New York Times</u> 1 Dec. 1997, late ed.: A20.

31. Review

Start with the name of the reviewer and the title of the review. Then insert *Rev. of* (for "Review of"), but do not underline it or enclose it in quotation marks. Next, provide the title of the piece reviewed, followed by a comma, the word *by*, and the name of the author of the piece being reviewed. If the name of the reviewer is not given, start with the title of the review; if no title is given either, start with *Rev. of*. End the entry with the name of the newspaper, magazine, or journal and the standard publication information.

Ribadeneira, Diego. "The Secret Lives of Seminarians." Rev. of <u>The New</u>

    <u>Men: Inside the Vatican's Elite School for American Priests</u>, by

    Brian Murphy. <u>Boston Globe</u> 31 Oct. 1997: C6.

32. Abstract from an Abstracts Journal

Begin by providing publication information on the original work. Then provide material on the journal in which you found the abstract: the title (underlined), the volume number, and the year (in parentheses), followed by a colon and the page or item number.

Johnson, Nancy Kay. "Cultural and Psychosocial Determinants of Health and

    Illness." Diss. U of Washington, 1980. <u>DAI</u> 40 (1980): 425B.

(*Diss.* means "Dissertation," and *DAI* is the abbreviation for *Dissertation Abstracts International*.)

Juliebo, Moira, et al. "Metacognition of Young Readers in an Early

    Intervention Reading Programme." Journal of Research in Reading 21.1

    (1998): 24-35. Psychological Abstracts 85.7 (1998): item 22380.

33. *Unsigned Article*

If an article has no known author, begin with its title, alphabetizing the citation by the first major word of the title on your references list.

"What You Don't Know About Desktops Can Cost You." Consumer Reports Sept.

    2002: 20-22.

Other Sources

34. *Film or Video Recording*

Begin with the film's title (underlined), followed by the director, distributor, and year of release; also provide other pertinent material, such as the names of the performers, writers, and producers, between the title and the name of the distributor.

Wayne's World. Dir. Penelope Spheeris. Prod. Lorne Michaels. Perf. Mike

    Myers, Dana Carvey, and Rob Lowe. Paramount, 1992.

35. *Television or Radio Program*

Provide the title of the episode (enclosed in quotation marks), if known; the title of the program (underlined); the title of the series (not underlined or enclosed in quotation marks), if any; the network; the call numbers or letters and local city, if any; and the date of broadcast.

"Commercializing Christians." All Things Considered. Natl. Public Radio.

    WBUR, Boston. 8 Dec. 1997.

"The Great Apes." National Geographic Special. PBS. WGBH, Boston. 12 July

    1984.

36. *Sound Recording*

For a sound recording that is available commercially, provide the name of the artist, the title of the recording (underlined, unless the piece is identified only by form, number, and key), the manufacturer, and the year of issue. Indicate the medium, if other than a compact disc, before the manufacturer's name.

```
Ball, Marica. Blue House. Rounder, 1994.

Ormandy, Eugene, cond. Symphony no. 3 in C minor, op. 78. By Camille

    Saint-Saëns. Perf. E. Power Biggs, organ. Philadelphia Orch. Sony,

    1991.

Raitt, Bonnie. "Something to Talk About." Luck of the Draw.

    Audiocassette. Capitol, 1991.
```

37. *Performance*

An entry for a play, concert, opera, or dance begins with the title (underlined), includes information similar to that given for a film, and ends with the performance site (for example, the theatre and city) and the date of the performance.

```
Blues for an Alabama Sky. By Pearl Cleage. Dir. Kenny Leon. Perf. Phylicia

    Rashad, Tyrone Mitchell Henderson, Sean C. Squire, Deidre N. Henry,

    and John Henry Redwood. Huntington Theatre, Boston. 5 Feb. 1997.
```

38. *Work of Art*

Provide the name of the artist, the title of the work (underlined), the name of the site that houses the work, and the city. If it is available, include the date the work was created immediately after the title. If the work is part of a private collection, provide the collector's name.

```
Cassatt, Mary. Breakfast in Bed. 1886. Private collection of Dr. and Mrs.

    John J. McDonough, Youngstown, OH.

---. Five O'Clock Tea. Museum of Fine Arts, Boston.
```

39. *Published Interview*

Provide the name of the person being interviewed; the title of the interview (enclosed in quotation marks), if any; the title of the source in which the interview is published; and any other pertinent bibliographic material.

Faulkner, William. "The Meaning of 'A Rose for Emily.'" Interview. 1959.

> The Story and Its Writer: An Introduction to Short Fiction. Ed.

> Ann Charters. Compact 4th ed. Boston: Bedford-St. Martin's, 1995.

> 772-73.

40. *Unpublished Interview*

Provide the name of the person being interviewed, the designation *Personal interview* (not underlined or in quotation marks), and the date of the interview.

Jensen, Steven. Personal interview. 12 Apr. 1997.

41. *Personal Letter to the Author*

Bush, George. Letter to the author. 8 Sept. 2002.

42. *Dissertation—Published*

Cite a published dissertation as a book, but add dissertation information before the publication data. Enclose the title of the dissertation in quotation marks, followed by the abbreviation *Diss.* (for "Dissertation"), the name of the degree-granting institution, a comma, and the year written.

Deatherage, Cynthia. A Way of Seeing: The Anglo-Saxons and the Primal

> World View. Diss. Purdue U, 1997. Ann Arbor: UMI, 1997. 9821728.

UMI stands for University Microfilms International. (For an example of a dissertation abstract citation, see page 52.)

43. *Dissertation—Unpublished*

Balkema, Sandra. "The Composing Activities of Computer Literate Writers."

> Diss. U of Michigan, 1984.

44. *Speech or Lecture*

Provide the name of the speaker; the title of the presentation (in quotation marks), if known; the meeting and sponsoring organization, if applicable; the place where the speech or lecture was given; and the date.

Booth, Wayne. "Ethics and the Teaching of Literature." College Forum.

> NCTE Convention. Cobo Center, Detroit. 21 Nov. 1997.

45. Map or Chart

Cite a map or a chart the same way you would cite a book with an unknown author, but add the label *Map* or *Chart* to distinguish it.

Wyoming. Map. Chicago: Rand, 1990.

46. Cartoon or Comic Strip

Schultz, Charles. "Peanuts." Cartoon. The Herald Journal 15 Aug. 2002: C6.

47. Advertisement

First name the item being advertised; then add the word *Advertisement* and supply the rest of the citation, indicating the source where the ad appeared.

Benadryl Severe Allergy & Sinus Headache. Advertisement. Prevention Sept.

2002: 55.

Electronic Media   Because electronic sources tend to be less perma-

WEBLINK
http://www.mla.org
MLA's Web site includes information about citing electronic media

nent and subject to fewer standards than printed works, their citations need more information than is required for print sources. Coverage of electronic references in MLA format is given in the sixth edition of the *MLA Handbook for Writers of Research Papers*, by Joseph Gibaldi (New York: MLA, 2003).

48. Entire Internet Site

Many times it is appropriate to reference an entire Internet Web site, such as a scholarly project or an information database. Include the information available at the site, in the following sequence:

1. The title of the site or project (underlined)
2. The creator or editor of the site (if given and relevant)
3. The electronic publication information: version number (if relevant), date of electronic publication or latest update, the name of the sponsoring organization or institution (if provided)
4. The date of access, and the URL within angle brackets

The Encyclopedia Mythica. Ed. M. F. Lindemans. 1995-2003. 3 Mar. 2003

    <http://www.pantheon.org/mythica>.

MSN.com. 2003. Microsoft Network. 28 Feb. 2003 <http://www.msn.com>.

Victoriana Online. Ed. Sylvania Dye. 1996-2002. 12 Jan. 2002

    <http://www.victorianaonline.com>.

To cite an anonymous article from a reference database, start with the title of the article (in quotation marks). Continue with the electronic publication information from the reference work. Be sure to give the unique address of the article you are citing if it is different from the URL for the database itself.

"Feather." _Britannica Online_. Vers. 98.1.1. May 1998. Encyclopedia

    Britannica. 12 Aug. 1998 <http://www.eb.com:175>.

49. Online Book

The complete texts of many books are now available online as well as in print. Provide the following items when citing such works:

1. The name of the author (if only an editor, compiler, or translator, is mentioned, give that person's name first, followed by *ed., comp.,* or *trans.*)
2. The title of the work, underlined
3. The name of any editor, compiler, or translator (if not given earlier)
4. Publication information from the printed work if the work has been printed
5. The date of electronic publication and the name of any sponsoring organization
6. The access date and the electronic address, in angle brackets

Woolf, Virginia. _The Voyage Out_. London: Faber, 1914. _The EServer_. Ed.

    Geoffrey Sauer, May 2003. U of Washington. 1 June 2003.

    <http://eserver.org/fiction/voyage-out.txt>.

When citing a part (chapter or section) of an online book, place the title or name of the part in quotation marks after the author's name. Be sure to give the URL of the specific part of the book if it is different from the complete book's URL.

Pope, Alexander. "Epistle I." Essay on Man. The EServer. Ed. Geoffrey

Sauer. 2003. U of Washington. 1 June 2003

<http://eserver.org/poetry/essay-on-man/epistle-i.txt>.

50. Article in an Online Periodical

Many magazines, newspapers, and scholarly journals are now available in online formats. Generally, citations for online periodicals follow the same sequence as citations for print periodicals. They should include the following:

1. The author's name, if provided
2. The title of the work, in quotation marks
3. The name of the journal, magazine, or newspaper, underlined
4. The volume and issue number (or other identifying number if provided)
5. The date of publication
6. The range or total number of pages, paragraphs, or sections, if they are numbered
7. The date of access and URL in angle brackets

51. Article in an Online Scholarly Journal

Reinhardt, Leslie Kaye. "British and Indian Identities in a

Picture by Benjamin West." Eighteenth Century Studies 31.3 (1998).

Project Muse. 12 July 1998 <http://muse.jhu.edu/journals/

eighteenth-century_studies>.

52. Article in an Online Newspaper or Magazine

Dedman, Bill. "Racial Bias Seen in U.S. Housing Loan Program."

New York Times on the Web 13 May 1998.

14 May 1998 <http://www.nytimes. com/archives>.

Ricks, Delthia. "Sickle Cell: New Hope." Newsday 12 May 1998. 12 May 1998

<http://www.newsday.com/homepage.htm>.

53. *Online Review*

Bast, Joseph L. Rev. of <u>Our Stolen Future</u>, by Theo Colborn et al.

    <u>Heartland Institute</u> 18 Apr. 1996: 27 pars. 25 June 1997

    <http://www.heartland.org/stolen1.htm>.

54. *Online Abstract*

Reid, Joy. "Responding to ESL Students' Tests." <u>TESOL Quarterly</u>

    28 (1994): 273-92. Abstract. 12 July 2000

    <http://vweb.wwilsonweb.com/cyi-bin/webspirs.cgi>.

55. *Online Editorial or Letter to the Editor*

"A Nuclear Threat from India." Editorial. <u>New York Times on the Web</u>

    13 May 1998. 14 May 1998 <http://www.nytimes.com/archives>.

Lowry, Heath. Letter. <u>Deseret News Online</u> 23 Mar. 1998. 25 Mar. 1998

    <http://www.desnews.com/archst.html>.

56. *Document Found Via an Information Database*

There are two commonly used types of online services: those to which users subscribe (e.g., AOL, Prodigy), and those to which libraries subscribe (e.g., Lexis-Nexis, ProQuest). If the service provides a URL for the source you are citing, follow the model for the appropriate online source as outlined above. That is, if the source you located via the online service is an online newspaper article, use the format for an online newspaper as given on p. 58. In such a case, there is no need to cite the online service itself. However, sometimes these services supply documents without providing a URL. For example, you may have located an item by using a keyword while in the database. If so, after providing the relevant information, provide the name of the online service, the date of access, and the keyword.

"Dr. Phil's Relationship Rescue." <u>Online With Oprah</u>. 12 July 2000.

    <u>America Online</u>. 15 Aug. 2000. Keyword: Oprah.

To cite online material without a URL that you derive from a service that your library subscribes to (e.g., Lexis-Nexis or ProQuest), follow the citation for the source itself with the name of the service (underlined), the library, and the date of access. If you know the URL of the service's home page, provide it in angle brackets at the end of the citation.

King, Marsha. "Companies Here Ponder Scout Ruling." Seattle Times 6 July

 2000: A1. Academic Universe. Lexis-Nexis. Utah State U Lib., Logan,

 UT. 15 Aug. 2000 <http://web.lexis-nexis.com/universe>.

57. Nonperiodical Publication on CD-ROM, Magnetic Tape, or Disc

Often, works on CDs, discs, or magnetic tape are published in a single edition, much as books are. To cite such publications, use a format similar to that used to cite books, with the addition of a description of the publication medium.

Corel WordPerfect Suite 8. CD-ROM. Ottawa, CA: Corel, 1998.

DeLorme Mapping. "Paris." Global Explorer. CD-ROM. Freeport, ME: DeLorme,

 1993.

(Note that DeLorme Mapping is the corporate author of this CD.)

"Symbolism." The Oxford English Dictionary. 2nd ed. CD-ROM. Oxford:

 Oxford UP, 1992.

58. Multidisc Publication

To cite a CD-ROM publication on multiple discs, list the number of discs or the specific number of the disc you used.

Great Literature Plus. CD-ROM, 4 discs. Parsippany: Bureau of Electronic

 Publishing, 1993.

59. Work in More than One Medium

When a work is published in more than one medium (for example, both as a book and as a CD or both as a CD and as a disc), you may specify all the media or only the medium you used.

Hult, Christine A., and Thomas N. Huckin. <u>The New Century Handbook</u>. 2nd
    ed. Book, CD-ROM. New York: Longman, 2002.

60. Electronic Television or Radio Program

Lifson, Edward. "Clinton Meets Kohl." <u>Morning Edition</u>. 13 May 1998.
    Natl. Public Radio. 20 June 1998 <http://www.npr.org/programs/
    morning/archives/1998>.

61. Electronic Sound Recording or Sound Clip

Beethoven, Ludwig van. "Symphony no. 5 in C, op. 67." June 1998. New City
    Media Audio Programs. 20 July 1998 <http://newcitymedia.com/
    radiostar/audio.htm>.

62. Electronic Film or Film Clip

Anderson, Paul Thomas, dir. <u>Boogie Nights</u>. 1997. Trailer. New Line
    Cinema. 13 May 1998 <http://hollywood.com>.

63. Email Communication

Provide the writer's name (or alias or screen name); the subject (title) of
the communication, if any (in quotation marks); the designation *Email to*;
the name of the person to whom the email is addressed; and the date of the
message.

Gillespie, Paula. "Members of the NWCA Board." Email to Michael
    Pemberton. 1 Aug. 1997.

Gardner, Susan. "Help with Citations." Email to the author. 20 Mar.
    1998.

64. Online Posting

In addition to the information provided for an email citation, a citation
for an online posting should include the description *Online posting* and the

date of the posting. Provide the name of the discussion list, if known. Then give the date of access. Last, provide the URL, if known, or the email address of the list's moderator or supervisor (in angle brackets).

```
Glennon, Sara. "Documenting Sessions." Online posting. 11 Dec. 1997.

    NWCA Discussion List. 12 Dec. 1997 <wcenter@ttacs6.ttu.edu>.
```

When possible, cite an archival version of the posting so that readers can more easily find and read the source:

```
White, Edward. "Texts as Scholarship: Reply to Bob Schwegler." Online

    posting. 11 Apr. 1997. WPA Discussion List. 12 Apr. 1997

    <http://gcinfo.gc.maricopa.edu/~wpa>.
```

Citation of a posting to a World Wide Web discussion forum follows the style for an online posting.

```
Hochman, Will. "Attention Paid This Sunday Morning." Online posting.

    5 Apr. 1998. Response to Selfe. 7 May 1998

    <http://www.ncte.org/forums/selfe/#forums>.
```

Citation of a posting to a Usenet newsgroup also follows the style for an online posting. Be sure to include the name of the newsgroup in angle brackets with the prefix *news*:

```
Shaumann, Thomas Michael. "Technical German." Online posting. 5 Aug.

    1994. 7 Sept. 1994 <news:comp.edu.languages.natural>.
```

65. Online Synchronous Communication

To cite an online synchronous communication, begin with the name (or alias or screen name) of the speaker, if available and if you are citing only one. Include a description of the event, the date of the event, the forum (for example, the name of the MOO), the access date, and the electronic address, preceded by *telnet://*.

```
Pine_Guest. Personal interview. 12 Dec. 1994. MediaMOO. 12 Dec. 1994.

    <telnet://moo.mediaMOO.com_7777>.
```

66. *Downloaded Computer Software*

<u>Fusion</u>. Vers. 1.1. 30 June 1998 <http://www.allaire.com>.

5e   Review a sample research paper in MLA format

The following research paper, written by Kaycee Sorensen, is formatted according to the MLA system of documentation. Annotations that explain various conventions are printed in blue.

Writer's last name and   **Sorensen 1**
page number appear
on every page.

Kaycee Sorensen   Student,
Professor Hult   professor,
English 2010H   course identification,
August 15, 2002   and date

Online Shopping: Title Centered
Risky (but Better) Business

Recently, I shopped at the Logan Old Navy to find a new pair   Double
of jeans, but since I wear an uncommon size, I could not find   spacing
exactly what I wanted. The attendant in the fitting rooms suggested
that I visit OldNavy.com to find what I was looking for. She gave   Introduction
using appeal
me all the information I would need to find the jeans and purchase   to authority
them online, and when I visited OldNavy.com, I found the jeans, and
they were cheaper than in the store. Needless to say, I bought more
than just the jeans because of the wonderful prices. This was not
my first experience, but because of the price, the convenience, and
access to more items, I became excited to seek out new online
shopping venues.

I am not alone in my growing interest in online shopping. According to <u>Nielsen-Netratings</u>, 498 million people worldwide now have access to the Internet from home, and just as these people are using the Internet for quick access to information and electronic communication, millions of them are also turning to the Internet for shopping purposes (Hupprich and Bumatay). Consumers should shop online because, despite fears of safety and identity theft, the simplicity, convenience of comparison-shopping, and access to a variety of merchandise makes online shopping the logical and best choice for consumers.

> Internet source without a page number

> Thesis: main point

The convenience of online shopping not only became clear to me as a consumer, but also as a retailer. During the holidays, I work for Sears in Frisco, TX. Our store is new and we still only serve the urban areas, so many people travel from rural areas to shop. While working over Christmas I helped one such woman who needed to shop for items for the baby she was expecting.

Sorensen 12

Works Cited   Alphabetical listing of all sources used

<u>Better Business Bureau Program</u>. 2002. 22 July 2002   Online: Professional site
    <www.bbbonline.org>.

Chan, Christine, et al. "Online Spending to Reach $10 Billion   Title of article
    for Holiday Season 2001." <u>Nielsen/NetRatings</u>

20 Nov. 2001. 28 July 2002 <http://www.nielsennetratings
.com/pr/pr_011022.pdf>.

Cox, Beth. "E-commerce: Color it Green." Cyberatlas 3
Aug. 2002. 12 Aug. 2002 <http://cyberatlas.internet.com/
markets/retailing/article/0,,6061_1364801,00.html>.

Frey, Christine. "Online Shopper: Advantages of Plastic."
Los Angeles Times 18 Oct. 2001: T8.

Greenspan, Robyn. "E-shopping Around the World." Cyberatlas
5 Aug. 2002. 23 Aug. 2002 <http://cyberatlas.internet.com/
markets/retailing/article/0,,6061_1431461,00.html>.

"How Encryption Works." Netscape Security Center. 5 Aug. 2002
<http://wp.netscape.com/security/basics/encryption.html>.

Hupprich, Laura, and Maria Bumatay. "Nielsen/Netratings Reports a
Record Half Billion People Worldwide Now Have Home Internet
Access." Nielsen/Netratings 3 June 2002. 3 Aug. 2002
<http://www.nielsen-netratings.com/pr/pr_020306_eratings.pdf>.

Kushairi, Ahmad. "The Buying Experience Is Still with Offline
Shopping." New Strait Times Press 12 Aug. 2002: 2.

"Nearly One-Third of Teens Make Offline Purchases after Window
Shopping Online." PR Newswire Association, Inc.
18 July 2001: Financial News Section. Academic Search
Elite. EBSCO. Utah State U Lib., Logan, UT. 20 Aug. 2002
<http://www.epnet.com>.

"Online-Shopping Safety and Security." The Shopping Guide 8 Aug. 2002.
12 Aug. 2002 <http://shoppingguide.hypermart.net/safety.html>.

Name of
professional site

Date of
publication

Date of access

Print:
Newspaper

Internet: Online
newsletter

Initial capitals
are used in
article titles,
which are also
put in quotation
marks.

Library reference
database: Full-
text article

Pastore, Michael. "Web Influences Offline Purchases, Especially
    Among Teens." <u>Cyberatlas</u> 3 Aug. 2002. 18 Aug. 2002
    <http://cyberatlas.internet.com/markets/retailing/article/
    0,,6061_804141,00.html>.

Stark, Ellen. "There's Help on the Way If You Face a Credit Card   Print:
    Dispute." <u>Money</u> May 1996: 41.   Magazine

"Virtual Model Tech Hikes Lands' End Sales." <u>Capital Times</u>
    27 Sept. 2001: 6E.

CHAPTER **6**

APA, CMS, and CBE Documentation

This chapter provides an overview of three styles of documentation, codified by the American Psychological Association, the *Chicago Manual of Style*, and the Council of Science Editors.

APA SYSTEM

The documentation system commonly employed in the social sciences was developed by the American Psychological Association (APA). Detailed documentation guidelines for the APA system are included in the *Publication Manual of the American Psychological Association*, 5th ed. (Washington, DC: APA, 2001). The social sciences use an author/date method of documentation.

In-text citations identify the source by the author's name and the date of publication so that the reader knows immediately whether the research cited is current. The date of publication is also emphasized in the References list at the end of the paper.

A Directory to the APA System

(Continued)

(Continued)

6a Integrate sources and avoid plagiarism in the APA system

In Chapter 3 "Evaluating and Using Sources: Avoiding Plagiarism," we talked in general about the importance of using sources accurately and responsibly in your research papers. To help you do so, the APA citation format provides for a two-part system of source identification: (1) parenthetical references within the body of the paper (discussed in 6b), and (2) a References list at the end of the paper (discussed in 6d). By using the APA system, you can integrate your source information appropriately and ethically without inadvertently committing plagiarism.

The APA Citation System

1. Introduce your source using a *signal phrase* that names its author, immediately followed by the date of publication in parentheses: Jones (1995) states that . . . .
2. Paraphrase or summarize the information from your source. It's best to use direct quotations sparingly. Rather, recast the source information into your own words. If you do use any words or

(Continued)

phrases from the author, however, be sure to include them in quotation marks and to provide a page number in parentheses.

3. If you did not name the author in a signal phrase, at the conclusion of your summary insert in parentheses the author's last name, a comma, and the date of publication: (Jones, 1995). For a direct quotation or close paraphrase, also provide a page number: (Jones, 1995, p. 75).

4. At the end of your paper, list the source with complete bibliographic information on your References page.

Plagiarism, a serious academic offense, is often committed by students inadvertently in the following two ways:

1. Failing to acknowledge a summary or paraphrase of a source in the body of the paper through a signal phrase and parenthetical citation.

2. Using the original authors' words without putting the borrowed words or phrases in quotation marks or including a parenthetical citation.

1 Acknowledge all sources

A successful research paper will be written as an argument in the writer's own words, expressing an understanding of the answers to specific research questions. In such a paper, sources are used as evidence in support of the writer's argument. Source support is integrated into the flow of the research paper through the use of paraphrases and summaries in the writer's own words; each source is acknowledged by a parenthetical citation. Failing to acknowledge a source results in plagiarism. In addition to paraphrases and summaries, any other source material must also be acknowledged, such as specific facts, graphics or visuals, cartoons, diagrams, or charts, using the two-part APA citation system. Note that the APA system stresses the publication date of a source by including that date in the parenthetical citation along with the name of the author. This custom has grown out of a desire of researchers in the social sciences to know immediately that the information found in a particular source is current and up to date.

2 Indicate original source words and phrases with quotation marks

The best research papers use direct quotations sparingly as support for their own ideas and integrate those quotations smoothly into the flow of the paper. A signal phrase alerts the reader that a direct quotation follows; the quotation marks show exactly which words and phrases are being quoted. Long quotations are formatted using indentation rather than quotation marks. Carelessness at the note-taking stage can result in unintentional plagiarism (see 3c).

6b Use the APA system for in-text citations

In the APA documentation system, reference citations found in the body of the paper are linked to the References list at the end. Both the author's last name and the year of publication are included in the in-text citation.

1. *Author Named in the Narrative*

If the author is mentioned in the narrative, provide the year of publication in parentheses just after the name.

```
Hacking (1995) covers much that is on public record about multiple
personality disorder.
```

2. *Author Not Named in the Narrative*

If the author is not mentioned in the narrative, provide the author's last name and the year of publication in parentheses at an appropriate place. Include a comma between the author's name and the date of publication.

```
In antiquity and through the middle ages, memory was a valued skill
(Hacking, 1995).
```

3. *Specific Page or Paragraph Quoted*

When quoting or directly paraphrasing the author's words, provide a page number (or a paragraph number if the electronic source includes one). Precede the page reference with the abbreviation *p.* (to cite one page), *pp.* (to cite more than one page), or the word *paragraph*.

```
There may be a causal explanation for multiple personality disorder,
because "multiplicity is strongly associated with early and repeated
child abuse, especially sexual abuse" (Hacking, 1995, p. 73).
```

If the quotation from an electronic source does not have pages or paragraph numbers, provide author and year only.

```
Vault Reports makes the following request on its Web site: "If you work
(or have worked) for a company we write about . . . please fill out our
Survey and tell us about your experience" (1998).
```

4. Work by Two Authors

In citing a work by two authors, provide the last names of both authors. Use the word *and* to separate their names in the narrative, but use an ampersand (&) to separate their names in an in-text parenthetical citation.

```
As Sullivan and Qualley (1994) point out, many recent publications
take the politics of writing instruction as their central
concern.
```

or

```
The explanation for recent turmoil in the academy may be found in
politics (Sullivan & Qualley, 1994).
```

5. Work by More than Two Authors

In the first reference to a work by three, four, or five authors, provide the last names for all authors. In subsequent citations, use the first author's last name and the Latin phrase *et al.* (for "and others"). When a work has six or more authors, include only the name of the first author, followed by *et al.*, in the first and in all following citations.

```
According to Britton et al. (1975), mature writers consider their readers
more than themselves.
```

6. Anonymous Work

If no author's name is provided, use either the title or an abbreviated form of the title (usually the first few words) for the in-text citation. Italicize the title of a book, periodical, brochure, or report; use quotation marks around the title of an article or chapter.

Public schools have become overly dependent on the IQ test as an indication of academic potential (*Human Abilities in Cultural Contexts*, 1988).

An individual's success in life depends in large measure on the cultural context in which he or she was raised ("Beyond IQ," 1994).

7. Work by a Corporate Author

Generally, provide the full name of a corporate author in in-text parenthetical citations.

Recently published statistics show the gap between the rich and poor to be widening (New York Times, Inc., 1996).

If the name of the corporate author is long (such as United Cerebral Palsy Association) or if its abbreviation is easily recognized (such as APA), use the abbreviation after including both the complete name and the abbreviation in the first text reference.

8. Works by Authors with the Same Last Name

When the reference list includes two or more primary authors with the same last name, provide those authors' initials in all citations, even if the publication dates are different.

G. A. Fraser (1990) writes about abuse as the cause of multiple personality disorder.

S. Fraser (1987) has written a memoir about incest and its effect on multiplicity.

9. *Two or More Sources*

To cite several different sources within the same parenthetical citation, list the sources in alphabetical order by the authors' names and use a semi-colon to separate the entries.

```
Several studies (Prinsky & Rosenbaum, 1987; Record Labeling, 1985;
Thigpen, 1993) show concern about songs with themes of drugs and violence.
```

10. *Personal Communication*

Personal correspondence, such as letters, telephone conversations, lecture notes, and email, should be cited only in the text itself. Do not list the communications on the References page because readers cannot access them. Provide the initials and the last name of the correspondent, the designation *personal communication,* and the date.

```
J. Tompkins suggests that fear of authority prevents true learning in
elementary, secondary, college, and university classrooms (personal
communication, August 7, 1997).
```

11. *Email Communication*

Email communication from individuals should be cited as personal communication within the text and is not included on the Works Cited list. The in-text citation is formatted as follows:

```
L. L. Meeks provided researchers with the pertinent information regarding
teacher training (personal communication, May 2, 2000).
```

12. *Web Sites*

When referring to an entire Web site (as opposed to a specific document or page on the site) it is sufficient in APA style to give the address of the Web site within the text itself. Such a reference is not included on the Works Cited page.

```
Patricia Jarvis's homepage includes a great deal of information about
recent archaeological digs in the Great Basin (http://www.asu.edu/
~students).
```

6c Format any content notes according to the APA system

The APA discourages use of content notes. They should be included only if they enhance or strengthen the discussion. Number notes consecutively throughout the text, using a superscript number. List the notes on a separate Notes page at the end of the text.

6d Format the References page according to the APA system

The research paper's References page (the equivalent of the Works Cited listing in MLA style) contains an alphabetical listing of all the works used as sources. The purpose of the References list is to help readers find the materials used in writing the paper, so the entries must be complete and accurate. List sources alphabetically by the last name of the author. When no author is given, alphabetize by the first word of the title (excluding *A, An,* or *The*). Format the References list in a paper according to the APA style for a final text: type the first word of each entry at the left margin and indent subsequent lines of the same entry five spaces (or one-half inch). Double-space the entire References page, both between and within entries.

Books A citation for a book has four basic parts:

Author's Name. (Publication Date). *Title of work.* Publication Information.

Begin a book citation with the author's last name, followed by a comma and the first and middle initials. Next include the year of publication, enclosed in parentheses and followed by a period. Italicize the title and subtitle of the book. Capitalize the first word of the title and the first word of the subtitle. Follow the title with publication information: the city of publication and the publisher, separated from each other with a colon. If the city is not well known or could be confused with another city, include a state or country abbreviation. Omit the word *Publisher* and abbreviations such as *Inc.* and *Co.* from the publisher's name. Include the complete names of university presses and associations. (For guidelines on citing books in electronic format, see page 84.)

1. Book by One Author

```
              Publication
Author        date                    Title of work
┌─────┐     ┌──────┐   ┌──────────────────────────────────────────┐
Bolick, C. (1988). Changing course: Civil rights at the crossroads.

     New Brunswick, NJ: Transaction Books.
     └──────────────────────────────────────────┘
              Publication information
```

2. Book by Two or More Authors

When a book has two to six authors, provide all the authors' names (last name first, followed by initials) in the order in which they appear on the title page. Note that this order may not be alphabetical. Connect the final two names with an ampersand (&). Abbreviate the seventh and subsequent authors as *et al.*

Hindelang, M. J., Hirschi, T., & Weis, J. G. (1981). *Measuring*

   delinquency. Beverly Hills, CA: Sage.

3. Book by a Corporate Author

Begin the entry with the full name of the group; alphabetize the entry by the first important word in the name. Should the same group be listed as author and publisher, include the word *Author* at the end of the entry in place of the publisher's name.

National Commission on Excellence in Education. (1984). *A nation at risk:*

   The full account. Cambridge, MA: USA Research.

4. Book with an Editor

For an edited book, provide the editor's name in place of an author's name. Include the abbreviation *Ed.* (for "Editor") or *Eds.* (for "Editors") in parentheses immediately following the editor's name.

Dilts, S. W. (Ed.). (1991). *Peterson's guide to four-year colleges*

   (21st ed.). Princeton, NJ: Peterson's Guides.

5. Chapter or Selection from an Edited Book

Start with the author's name, the year of publication, and the title of the selection. Do not underline the title or enclose it in quotation marks. Next, provide the names of the editors in normal order as they appear on the title page, preceded by the word *In* and followed by the abbreviation *Ed.* or *Eds.* (in parentheses). End the entry with the book's title (underlined), the inclusive page numbers for the selection (in parentheses), and the publication information.

Kadushin, A. (1988). Neglect in families. In E. W. Nunnally,

    C. S. Chilman, & F. M. Cox (Eds.), *Mental illness, delinquency,*

    addiction, and neglect (pp. 147-166). Newbury Park, CA: Sage.

6. *Two or More Books by the Same Author*

Arrange the entries by the date of publication, with the earliest first. If you have two or more works by the same author published in the same year, alphabetize by title and distinguish the entries by adding a lowercase letter immediately after the year: (1991a), (1991b).

Flynn, J. R. (1980). *Race, IQ, and Jensen.* London: Routledge.

Flynn, J. R. (1991). *Asian Americans: Achievement beyond IQ.* Hillsdale,

    NJ: Erlbaum.

7. *Article in a Reference Book*

If an encyclopedia entry is signed, start with the author's name; if it is unsigned, start with the title of the article. The publication date follows the author's name or, if no author's name is given, the title of the article. Provide the volume number and page numbers of the article (in parentheses) after the title of the reference book.

Davidoff, L. (1984). Childhood psychosis. In *The encyclopedia of*

    psychology (Vol. 10, pp. 156-157). New York: Wiley.

8. *Book in Translation*

Indicate the name of the translator in parentheses after the book's title, with the abbreviation *Trans.*

Freire, P. (1993). *Pedagogy of the oppressed* (New rev. 20th anniv. ed.,

    M. B. Ramos, Trans.). New York: Continuum.

9. Subsequent Edition of a Book

If a book is not a first edition, indicate the relevant edition in parentheses immediately following the title of the book. Use abbreviations to specify the type of edition: for example, *2nd ed.* stands for "Second edition" and *Rev. ed.* stands for "Revised edition."

Lindeman, E. (1987). *A rhetoric for writing teachers* (2nd ed.). New York:

   Oxford University Press.

10. Republished Book

Provide the original date of publication in parentheses at the end of the entry, with the words *Original work published*.

Dewey, J. (1963). *Experience and education.* New York: Collier. (Original

   work published 1938)

11. Government Document

Unless an author's name is given, begin an entry for a government document with the name of the agency that issued the publication.

National Center for Educational Statistics. (1996). *The condition of*

   education 1996. Washington, DC: U.S. Department of Education, Office

   of Educational Research and Improvement.

12. Published Proceedings from a Conference

Van Belle, J. G. (2002). Online interaction: Learning communities in the

   virtual classroom. In J. Chambers (Ed.), *Selected Papers from the*

   13th International Conference on College Teaching and Learning (pp.

   187-200). Jacksonville, FL: Community College at Jacksonville Press.

13. One Volume of a Multivolume Work

Doyle, A. C. (1930). *The complete Sherlock Holmes* (Vol. 2). Garden City:

   Doubleday.

Periodicals A citation of an article in a periodical or a journal follows a format similar to that for a book:

Author's name. (Publication date). Article title. Publication information.

When citing magazines and newpapers, include the month and date of publication. The article title and subtitle appear without quotation marks or italics. The publication information begins with the name of the publication as it appears on the publication's title page, with all major words capitalized. Italicize the journal name. Include the volume number (italicized and not preceded by the abbreviation *vol.*) and the issue number (in parentheses and not italicized) for journals that are not numbered consecutively throughout the volume. End with the inclusive page numbers for the article. (Use the abbreviation *p.* or *pp.* with articles in newspapers but not with articles in journals or magazines.) (For guidelines on citing articles in online periodicals, see page 85.)

14. Article in a Journal Paginated by Volume

Popenoe, D. (1993). American family decline, 1960-1990: A review and

appraisal. *Journal of Marriage and Family, 55,* 527-555.

Author | Publication date | Article title | Article subtitle

Publication information

15. Article in a Journal Paginated by Issue

If each issue of a journal begins with page 1, provide the issue number (in parentheses) immediately following the volume number.

Alma, C. (1994). A strategy for the acquisition of problem-solving

expertise in humans: The category-as-analogy approach. *Inquiry,*

14(2), 17-28.

16. Article in a Monthly Magazine

Include the month, not abbreviated, following the year in the publication date.

Katz, L. G. (1994, November). Perspectives on the quality of early

childhood programs. *Phi Delta Kappan, 76,* 200-205.

17. Article in a Weekly Magazine

Provide the year, month, and day of publication.

Ives, D. (1994, August 14). Endpaper: The theory of anything. *The New York Times Magazine*, 58.

If the article has no known author, start the entry with the title of the article, and alphabetize by the first important word in the title (usually the word that follows the introductory article).

The blood business. (1972, September 7). *Time*, 47-48.

In the References list, this entry would appear in the B's.

18. Newspaper Article

Provide the complete name of the newspaper (including any introductory articles) after the title of the article. List all discontinuous page numbers, preceded by *p.* or *pp.*

Fritz, M. (1992, November 7). Hard-liners to boycott German anti-racism rally. *The Dallas Morning News*, pp. 1, 25.

19. Editorial

Add the word *Editorial*, in brackets, after the title of the editorial.

Paglia, C. (1997, October 24). More mush from the NEA [Editorial]. *The Wall Street Journal*, p. A22.

20. Letter to the Editor

Add the designation *Letter to the editor*, in brackets, after the title of the letter or after the date if there is no title.

Schack, S. (1997, December 1). [Letter to the editor]. *The New York Times*, p. A20.

21. Review

Provide the name of the reviewer, the date of publication (in parentheses), and the title of the review, if given. Then, in brackets, write the designation *Review of* and the title of the piece that was reviewed.

Ribadeneira, D. (1997, October 31). The secret lives of seminarians
    [Review of the book *The new men: Inside the Vatican's elite school
    for American priests*]. *The Boston Globe*, p. C6.

22. Unsigned article

Quacks in European solidarity (2002, August). *The Economist*, 50.

23. More Than One Work by the Same Author in the Same Year

List the works alphabetically by title and use the lowercase letters *a, b, c,*
etc. after the dates to distinguish the works.

Hayles, N. K. (1996a). Inside the teaching machine: Actual feminism and
    (virtual) pedagogy. *The Electronic Journal for Computer Writing,
    Rhetoric and Literature, 2*. Retrieved Nov. 15, 1996, from
    http://www.cwrl.utexas.edu/cwrl

Hayles, N. K. (1996b). Self/Subject. In P. Vandenberg & P. Heilker
    (Eds.), *Keywords in composition* (pp. 217-220). Portsmouth, NH:
    Heinemann/Boynton-Cook.

Other Sources

24. Film or Video Recording

Begin with the names of those responsible for the film and, in parentheses, their titles, such as *Producer* and *Director*. Give the title (italicized), and
then designate the medium in brackets. Provide the location and the name of
the distributor.

Rosenthal, J., et al. (Producers), & Ramis, H. (Director). (2002).
    Analyze That [Motion Picture]. Hollywood: Warner Brothers.

25. Television or Radio Program

Identify those who created the program, and give their titles—for example, *Producer, Director,* and *Anchor.* Give the date the program was broadcast.

Provide the program's title (italicized), as well as the city and the station where the program aired.

Miller, R. (Producer). (1982, May 21). *Problems of freedom.* New York:

    NBC-TV.

26. *Technical Report*

Write an entry for a technical report in a format similar to that for a book. If an individual author is named, provide that information; place any other identifying information (such as a report number) after the title of the report.

Vaughn Hansen Associates, in association with CH2M Hill and Water

    Research Laboratory, Utah State University. (1995). *Identification*

    and assessment of certain water management options for the Wasatch

    Front: Prepared for Utah State Division of Water Resources. Salt

    Lake City, UT: Author.

27. *Published Interview*

For a published interview, start with the name of the interviewer and the date. In brackets, give the name (and title, if necessary) of the person interviewed. End with the publication information, including the page number(s), in parentheses, after the title of the work in which the interview is published.

Davidson, P. (1992). [Interview with Donald Hall]. In P. Davidson, *The*

    fading smile (p. 25). New York: Knopf.

28. *Unpublished Interview*

Follow the format for a published interview.

Hult, C. (1997, March). [Interview with Dr. Stanford Cazier, past

    President, Utah State University].

29. *Unpublished Dissertation*

Provide the author's name, the date, and then the title of the dissertation, italicized and followed by a period. Add the phrase *Unpublished doctorial dissertation,* a comma, and the name of the degree-granting institution.

Johnson, N. K. (1980). *Cultural and psychological determinants of health
    and illness.* Unpublished doctoral dissertation, University of
    Washington.

30. Speech or Lecture

For an oral presentation, provide the name of the presenter, the year and
month of the presentation, and the title of the presentation (italicized). Then
give any useful location information.

Meeks, L. (1997, March). *Feminism and the WPA.* Paper presented at
    the Conference on College Composition and Communication,
    Phoenix, AZ.

31. Paper Presented at a Conference

Provide information about the location of the meeting as well as the
month in which the meeting was held.

Klaus, C. (1996, March). *Teachers and writers.* Paper presented at the
    meeting of the Conference on College Composition and Communication,
    Milwaukee.

Electronic Media   The Fifth Edition
of the *Publication Manual of the American
Psychological Association* (2001) provides
new formats for electronic documentation,
shown below. When citing electronic media,
use the standard APA format to identify au-
thorship, date of origin (if known), and title,
much as for print material; the Web information is placed in a retrieval statement at

WEBLINK

http://www.apa.org
The official Web site of the
American Psychological
Association

the end of the reference. If you are referencing an electronic version that du-
plicates exactly a print source, simply use the basic journal reference format
for print sources. Indicate the electronic version by including the terms
[Electronic Version] in brackets immediately following the article's title.

32. Online Professional or Personal Site

To comply with APA style, present information in the following general sequence when citing online sources:

1. The author's or editor's last name and initial(s)
2. The creation date of the work, in parentheses; use *n.d.* (no date) if the electronic publication date is not available
3. The title of the complete work, italicized
4. The relevant subpage (if the document is contained within a large, complex site)
5. The phrase "Retrieved (date) from" http:
6. The access protocol or path or URL. (Note: Only break URL lines after a slash or before a period; do not follow the URL with a period.)

Jarvis, P. (n.d.). *My Homepage.* Retrieved December 3, 1997, from

  http://www.mtu.edu/~students

McCarthy, B. (1997). *Reflections on the past--Antiques.* Retrieved

  January 20, 1998, from Resources for Victorian Living Web site:

  http://www.victoriana.com

33. Online Book

Provide any data on the print publication before giving details on where the electronic version may be located.

Aristotle. (1954). *Rhetoric* (W. R. Roberts, Trans.). Retrieved

  April 8, 1997, from *The English Server* at Carnegie

  Mellon University: http://www.rpi.edu/~honeyl/Rhetoric/

  index.html

34. Article in an Online Work

Generally, citations for articles in online works follow the same sequence as citations for their print counterparts.

Women in American history. (1998). In *Encyclopaedia Britannica.*

  Retrieved May 25, 1998, from http://www.women.eb.com

35. Article in a Daily Online Newspaper or on a Newswire

Schmitt, E. (1988, February 4). Cohen promises "significant" military
    campaign against Iraq if diplomacy fails. *The New York Times on the*
    Web. Retrieved from http://www.nytimes.com/archives

(Note: No need to repeat the date of retrieval if it is the same as the publication date.)

36. Article in an Online Magazine

Thakker, S. (1998, May). Avoiding automobile theft. *Ontario Police Crime*
    Prevention Magazine. Retrieved May 26, 1998, from
    http://www.opcpm.com/inside/avoidingautomobile.html

37. Online Review

Spiers, S. (1998). [Review of the report "Blood poisoning" by
    Prevention/NBCToday.] *OBGYN.net.* Retrieved August 3, 1998, from
    http://www.obgyn.net/women/articles

38. Online Abstract

Reid, J. (1983). Computer-assisted text-analysis for ESL students. *Calico*
    Journal, 1(3), 40-42. Abstract retrieved August 2, 1998, from DIALOG
    database (ERIC Item: EJ29870).

39. Online Editorial or Letter to the Editor

Spilner, M. (1998, May). Walking club welcome [Editorial]. *Prevention.*
    Retrieved June 20, 1998, from http://www.prevention.com/walking/
    welcome.html

Rivel, D. (1998, May 6). Art in the schools [Letter to editor].
    The New York Times on the Web. Retrieved May 6, 1998, from
    http://www.nytimes.com/yr/mo/day/letters

40. Article in an Online Scholarly Journal

Britt, R. (1995). The heat is on: Scientists agree on human contribution

to global warming. *Ion Science.* Retrieved November 13, 1996, from

http://www.injersey.com/Media/IonSci/features/gwarm

41. Document or Full-Text Article Found Via a Reference Database

To cite a full-text article you derive from a service that your library subscribes to (e.g., *Lexis-Nexis, EbscoHost,* or *ProQuest*), follow the citation for the
source itself (the same as for its print counterpart) with the name of the service (underlined) and the library. Provide the date of access and the URL of the
service's home page in a retrieval statement.

King, M. (2000, July 6). Companies here ponder scout ruling. *Seattle*

Times, A1. Lexis-Nexis. Utah State U. Library, Logan, UT. Retrieved

August 15, 2000, from http://web.lexis-nexis.com/universe

42. Nonperiodical Publication on CD-ROM, Magnetic Tape, or Disk

ClearVue, Inc. (1995). *The history of European literature* [CD-ROM].

Chicago: Author.

43. Online Interview

Jorgenson, L. (1998, May 26). For a change, Jazz feel bullish [Interview

with Jeff Hornacek]. *Deseret News,* 15 paragraphs. Retrieved May 27,

1998, from http://www.desnews.com/playoffs

44. Online Posting

Although unretrievable communication such as email is not included in
APA References, public or retrievable Internet postings from newsgroups or
listservs may be included.

Shaumann, T. (1994, August 5). Technical German. *Technical German*

Discussion List. Retrieved September 7, 1994, from

USENET@comp.edu.languages.natural

45. *Online Synchronous Communication*

WorldMOO Computer Club. (1988, February 3). Monthly meeting. Retrieved

    February 3, 1998 from telnet:world.sensemedia.net1234

6e Review a sample research report in APA format

The following research paper, written by two students in a general education course, is formatted according to the APA system of documentation. Annotations that explain various conventions are included in the margins.

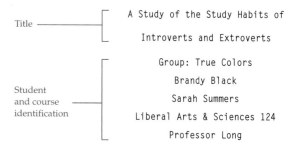

Title page   Shortened title appears with   Introverts and Extroverts   1
                 page number on every page

Running Head: INTROVERTS AND EXTROVERTS
If the paper is being submitted for publication, include the shortened
title to be used as a header on every page of the printed version

Title ———   A Study of the Study Habits of

             Introverts and Extroverts

               Group: True Colors

                 Brandy Black

Student
and course ———   Sarah Summers
identification
         Liberal Arts & Sciences 124

                Professor Long

             October 30, 2002

An abstract, a brief summary of the
paper, is often included as the second
page in social science papers.

A Study of the Study Habits of
Introverts and Extroverts

Title

Research about personality types and their study habits has
become increasingly important. In particular, psychologists have
studied how to recognize personality types of students and how to
teach different kinds of students. Because of this national
interest, we decided to investigate the study habits of two
personality types, introverts and extroverts. We began this study
with two general assumptions. First, we thought that introverts
would be less socially active in their study habits, spend more
time studying, and have a higher degree of academic success.
Second, we thought that extroverts would study in groups, study
less, and have slightly lower grades. In order to investigate
our assumptions, we read several articles in journals such as
Psychological Reports, Personality and Individual Differences,
and *The Journal of Research in Personality.*

Double-spaced text

— Hypothesis

Background information

We constructed a four-page survey about academic success and
study habits which we asked fifteen students to answer. In
addition, we also created a six-day study log to chart the length
of study time, duration of breaks, and types of studying done by
the students. The purpose of this research report is to review the
literature and to present information from our own research. This
report shows that our own research, for the most part, replicated
the findings of many of the national studies. Information in this

— Thesis

paper will be presented in two sections. First, findings from the larger, national studies will be summarized. Then, findings from our study will follow.

> Others' research is reviewed and summarized in the literature review

Literature Review

According to national studies, there are three major trends used in tracing the academic life of extroverts and introverts.

APA citation style

Only first word and proper nouns are capitalized in article or book title

Introverts and Extroverts   6

Initials

References

Campbell, J. B. (1983). Differential relationships of extroversion, impassivity, and sociability to study habits. *Journal of* — Publication date *Research in Personality, 17,* 308-313. ——— Page numbers

Campbell, J. B., & Hawley, C. W. (1982). Study habits and Eysenck's theory of extroversion-introversion. *Journal of Research in* Journal name, *Personality, 16,* 139-146.

> in capital and lowercase letters, is italicized

Furnham, A., & Medhurst, S. (1995). Personality correlates of academic seminar behavior: A study of four instruments. *Personality and Individual Differences, 19,* 197-208.

> No quotation marks around title

Irfani, S. (1978). Extroversion-introversion and self-rated academic success. *Psychological Reports, 43,* 505-510.

> Volume number is italicized

Olympia, D. E., Sheridan, S. M., Jenson, W. R., & Andrews, D. (1994). Using student-managed interventions to increase homework completion and accuracy. *Journal of Applied Behavior*

> Internet journal

Analysis, 27, 88-99. Retrieved September 25, 1998, from

http://www.envmed.rochester.edu/www.rap/behavior/jaba.htm

CMS SYSTEM

The documentation system used most commonly in business, communications, economics, and the humanities and fine arts (other than languages and literature) is outlined in *The Chicago Manual of Style,* 15th ed. (Chicago: The University of Chicago Press, 2003). This two-part system uses footnotes or

WEBLINK

http://www.press.uchicago
.edu/Misc/Chicago/cmosfaq
.html
For answers to questions
about CMS style

endnotes and a bibliography to provide publication information about sources quoted, paraphrased, summarized, or otherwise referred to in the text of a paper. Footnotes appear at the bottom of the page; endnotes appear on a separate page at the end of the paper. The Bibliography, like the Works Cited page in the MLA documentation style, is an alphabetical list of all works cited in the paper.

6f Integrate sources and avoid plagiarism in the CMS system

In Chapter 3, "Evaluating and Using Sources: Avoiding Plagiarism," we talked in general about the importance of using sources accurately and responsibly in your research papers. To help you do so, the CMS citation format provides for a two-part system of source identification: (1) footnote superscript numbers and footnotes within the body of the paper (discussed in 6g and h), and (2) a Bibliography at the end of the paper (discussed in 6i). By using the CMS system, you can integrate your source information appropriately and ethically without inadvertently committing plagiarism.

The CMS Citation System

1. Introduce your source using a *signal phrase* that names its author, with a superscript footnote number following the source information: Jones states that. . . .[1]
2. Paraphrase or summarize the information from your source. It's best to use direct quotations sparingly. Rather, recast the source information into your own words. If you do use any words or phrases from the author, however, be sure to include them in quotation marks.
3. Format your footnotes (which are listed on the page on which the source was cited) or endnotes (which are typed in one consecutive list at the end of the paper before the bibliography) according to the CMS style.
4. At the end of your paper, list the source with complete bibliographic information on your Bibliography page.

Plagiarism, a serious academic offense, is often committed by students inadvertently in the following two ways:

1. Failing to acknowledge a summary or paraphrase of a source in the body of the paper through a signal phrase and parenthetical citation.
2. Using the original authors' words without putting the borrowed words or phrases in quotation marks or including a parenthetical citation.

1 Acknowledge all sources

A successful research paper will be written as an argument in the writer's own words, expressing an understanding of the answers to specific research questions. In such a paper, sources are used as evidence in support of the writer's argument. Source support is integrated into the flow of the research paper through the use of paraphrases and summaries in the writer's own words; each source is acknowledged by a parenthetical citation. Failing to acknowledge a source results in plagiarism. In addition to paraphrases and summaries, any other source material must also be acknowledged, such as specific facts, graphics or visuals, cartoons, diagrams, or charts, using the CMS footnote citation system.

2 Indicate original source words and phrases with quotation marks

The best research papers use direct quotations sparingly as support for their own ideas and integrate those quotations smoothly into the flow of the paper. A signal phrase alerts the reader that a direct quotation follows; the quotation marks show exactly which words and phrases are being quoted. Long quotations are formatted using indentation rather than quotation marks. Carelessness at the note-taking stage can result in unintentional plagiarism (see 3c).

6g Use the CMS system for in-text citations

In the text, indicate a note with a superscript number typed immediately after the information that is being referenced. Number notes consecutively throughout the text.

In A History of Reading, Alberto Manguel asserts that "we, today's readers, have yet to learn what reading is."[1] As a result, one of his conclusions is that while readers have incredible powers, not all of them are enlightening.[2]

6h Format notes according to the CMS system

For footnotes, position the text of the note at the bottom of the page on which the reference occurs. Separate the footnotes from the text by skipping four lines from the last line of text. Single-space within a note, but double-space between notes if more than one note appears on a page.

For endnotes, type all of the notes at the end of the paper, in a section entitled Notes. The title, centered but not in quotation marks, should appear at the top of the first page of the notes. List the notes in consecutive order, as they occur in the text. Double-space the entire endnote section—between and within entries.

The other details of formatting are the same for both footnotes and endnotes. Indent the first line of each note five spaces (or one-half inch). Use a number that is the same size as and is aligned in the same way as the note text (do not use a superscript); follow the number with a period and a word space to the note itself. Begin with the author's name (first name first), followed by a comma. Then provide the title of the book (underlined or italicized) or article (enclosed in quotation marks). Finally, provide the publication information. For books, include (in parentheses) the place of publication, followed by a colon; the publisher, followed by a comma; and the date of publication. Conclude with the page number of the source, preceded by a comma. For articles, include the title of the periodical (underlined or italicized), followed by the volume or issue number. Then add the date of publication (in parentheses), followed by a colon and the page number.

BOOK

1. Alberto Manguel, A History of Reading (New York: Viking, 1996), 23.

ARTICLE

2. Steven Brachlow, "John Robinson and the Lure of Separatism in Pre-Revolutionary England," Church History 50 (1983): 288-301.

In subsequent references to the same source, it is acceptable to use only the author's last name and a page number:

3. Manguel, 289.

Where there are two or more works by the same author, include a shortened version of each work's title:

4. Merton, Mystics, 68.

Books

Book by One Author

5. Iris Murdoch, The Sovereignty of Good (New York: Schocken Books, 1971), 32-33.

Book by Two or Three Authors

List the authors' names in the same order as on the title page of the book.

6. Anne S. Goodsell, Michelle R. Maher, and Vincent Tinto, Collaborative Learning: A Sourcebook for Higher Education (University Park, Pa.: National Center on Postsecondary Teaching, Learning, and Assessment, 1992), 78.

Book by More than Three Authors

In the note itself, use the abbreviation *et al.* after the first author's name; list all authors in the accompanying bibliography entry.

7. James Britton et al., The Development of Writing Abilities (London: Macmillan, 1975), 43.

Book by a Corporate Author

8. American Association of Colleges and Universities, American Pluralism and the College Curriculum: Higher Education in a Diverse Democracy (Washington, D.C.: American Association of Higher Education, 1995), 27.

Book with an Editor

9. Jane Roberta Cooper, ed., Reading Adrienne Rich: Review and Re-Visions, 1951-1981 (Ann Arbor: University of Michigan Press, 1984), 51.

Book with an Editor and an Author

10. Albert Schweitzer, <u>Albert Schweitzer: An Anthology</u>, ed. Charles R. Joy (New York: Harper & Row, 1947), 107.

Chapter or Selection from an Edited Work

11. Gabriele Taylor, "Gossip as Moral Talk," in <u>Good Gossip</u>, ed. Robert F. Goodman and Aaron Ben-Ze'ev (Lawrence: Kansas University Press, 1994), 35-37.

Article in a Reference Book

The publication information (city of publication, publisher, publication year) is usually omitted from citations of well-known reference books. Include the abbreviation *s. v.* (*sub verbo,* or "under the word") before the article title, rather than page numbers.

12. Frank E. Reynolds, <u>World Book Encyclopedia</u>, 1983 ed., s. v. "Buddhism."

Introduction, Preface, Foreword, or Afterword

13. Jane Tompkins, preface to <u>A Life in School: What the Teacher Learned</u> (Reading, Mass.: Addison-Wesley, 1996), xix.

Work in More than One Volume

14. Arthur Conan Doyle, <u>The Complete Sherlock Holmes</u>, vol. 2 (Garden City, N.Y.: Doubleday, 1930), 728.

Government Document

15. United States Federal Bureau of Investigation, <u>Uniform Crime Reports for the United States: 1995</u> (Washington, D.C.: GPO, 1995), 48.

Periodicals

Article in a Journal Paginated by Volume

16. Mike Rose, "The Language of Exclusion: Writing Instruction at the University," College English 47 (1985): 343.

Article in a Journal Paginated by Issue

17. Joy S. Ritchie, "Confronting the 'Essential' Problem: Reconnecting Feminist Theory and Pedagogy," Journal of Advanced Composition 10, no. 2 (1989): 160.

Article in a Monthly Magazine

18. Douglas H. Lamb and Glen D. Reeder, "Reliving Golden Days," Psychology Today, June 1986, 22.

Article in a Weekly Magazine

19. Steven Levy, "Blaming the Web," Newsweek, 7 April 1997, 46-47.

Newspaper Article

20. P. Ray Baker, "The Diagonal Walk," Ann Arbor News, 16 June 1928, sec. A, p. 2.

Abstract from an Abstracts Journal

21. Nancy K. Johnson, "Cultural and Psychological Determinants of Health and Illness" (Ph.D. diss., University of Washington, 1980), abstract in Dissertation Abstracts International 40 (1980): 425B.

Other Sources

Speech or Lecture

22. Wayne Booth, "Ethics and the Teaching of Literature" (paper presented to the College Forum at the 87th Annual Convention of the National Council of Teachers of English, Detroit, Mich., 21 November 1997).

Personal Letter to the Author

23. George Bush, letter to author, 8 September 1995.

Electronic Media The latest edition of the *Chicago Manual of Style* (15th edition, 2003), covers formats for electronic media far more thoroughly than did the previous (14th) edition. The latest edition specifically addresses the advent of electronic sources and integrates its coverage of electronic documentation formats with coverage of print citations. In general, electronic sources are cited much as print sources are cited. The URL is listed at the end of the citation and is not placed in angle brackets. CMS points out that dates of access are of limited usefulness because of the changeable nature of electronic sources. They suggest using the date of access only in fields where the information is particularly time-sensitive, such as medicine or law. If an access date is needed, place it in parentheses following the URL as in the example from an online law journal below:

24. Ruthe Catolico Ashley, "Creating the Ideal Lawyer," New Lawyer, April 3, 2003, http://www.abanet.org/genpractice/newlawyer/april03/ideal.html (accessed July 20, 2003).

Online Professional or Personal Site

25. Academic Info., 1998-2000, "Humanities," http://www.academicinfo.net/ index.html.

26. Michelle Traylor, "Michelle Traylor Data Services," 1989-2002, http://www.mtdsnet.com.

27. John C. Herz, "Surfing on the Internet: A Nethead's Adventures Online," Urban Desires 1.3, March/April 1995, http://www.desires.com.

6i Format bibliography entries according to the CMS system

The style for Bibliography entries is generally the same as that for Works Cited entries in MLA style. Follow the formatting conventions outlined in Chapter 5 when creating a Bibliography page.

CBE SYSTEM

Although source citations in the sciences are generally similar to those recommended by the APA, there is no uniform system of citation in the sciences. Various disciplines follow either the style of a particular journal or the style outlined in a style guide, such as the guide produced by the Council of Biology Editors: *Scientific Style and Format: The CBE Manual for Authors, Editors, and Publishers*, 6th ed. (New York: Cambridge University Press, 1994).

The Council of Biology Editors (CBE) became the Council of Science Editors on January 1, 2000. The new name, which was voted on by the membership during 1999, more accurately re-

WEBLINK

http://councilscienceeditors.org

The official Web site of the Council of Science Editors

flects its expanding membership. CBE was established in 1957 by joint action of the National Science Foundation and the American Institute of Biological Sciences. More information about the organization can be found at their Web site (listed in the box).

6j Integrate sources and avoid plagiarism in the CBE system

In Chapter 3 "Evaluating and Using Sources: Avoiding Plagiarism," we talked in general about the importance of using sources accurately and responsibly in your research papers. To help you do so, the CBE citation format provides for a two-part system of source identification: (1) parenthetical references or reference numbers within the body of the paper (discussed in 6k), and (2) a References list that is either alphabetical or numerical at the end of the paper (discussed in 6l). By using the CBE system, you can integrate your source information appropriately and ethically without inadvertently committing plagiarism. Since the CBE citation system closely resembles the APA system, for more on integrating sources and avoiding plagiarism please see the information in 6a on pages 69–71.

6k Use the CBE system for in-text citations

The CBE system of documentation offers two alternative formats for in-text citations: the name-year (or author-year) system and the citation sequence (or number).

Name-Year System If the author's name is used to introduce the source material, include only the publication date in the citation.

> According to Allen (1997), frequency
> of interactions and context of occurrence
> were unknown.

WEBLINK

http://www.wisc.edu/
writing/Handbook/
DocCBE_NameYear_Intext
.html

A basic outline of the CBE's name-year system for in-text citation

  or

> Frequency of interactions and context of occurrence were unknown
> (Allen 1997).

Note that there is no comma between author and year in CBE style.

Citation Sequence System In the citation sequence system, numbers are assigned to the various sources, according to the sequence in which the sources are initially cited in the text. Then the sources are listed by number on the References page. Set citation numbers within the text as superscripts.

> Temperature plays a major role in the rate of gastric juice secretion.[3]

Multiple sources are cited together:

> Recent studies[3,5,8-10] show that antibodies may also bind to microbes
> and prevent their attachment to epithelial surfaces.

6l Format the References page for the citation sequence in CBE style

Like the MLA's Works Cited page, the CBE's listing of references contains all the sources cited in the paper. The title of this page may be References or

Cited References. Since the purpose of this list is to help readers find the materials used in writing the paper, information must be complete and accurate.

The format of the References page will depend on whether the name-year system or the citation sequence system is used. Since the References page for the CBE name-year system basically resembles the APA References page discussed in 6d, we will consider here the References page for the citation sequence system.

Double-space the entire References list, both between and within entries. Type the citation number, followed by a period, flush left on the margin. Leave two word spaces to the first letter of the entry. Align any turn lines on the first letter of the entry. List the citations in order of appearance in the text.

List authors with last names first, followed by initials. Capitalize only the first word of a title and any proper nouns. Do not enclose titles of articles in quotation marks, and do not underline titles of books or journals. Abbreviate names of journals, where possible. Include the year of publication. Cite volume and page numbers when appropriate.

(Note that initial numerals accompany citations in the list *only* when the citation sequence system is used. The citations appear in alphabetical order when the name-year system is used.)

Books

Book by One Author

1. Kruuk H. The spotted hyena: a study of predation and social behavior. Chicago: University of Chicago Pr; 1972.

2. Abercrombie MLJ. The anatomy of judgment. Harmondsworth (Eng.): Penguin; 1969.

Book by Two or More Authors

3. Hersch RH, Paolitto DP, Reimer J. Promoting moral growth. New York: Longman; 1979.

Book by a Corporate Author

4. Carnegie Council on Policy Studies in Higher Education. Fair practices in higher education: rights and responsibilities of

students and their colleges in a period of intensified competition for enrollment. San Francisco: Jossey-Bass; 1979.

Book with Two or More Editors

5. Buchanan RE, Gibbons NE, editors. Bergey's manual of determinative bacteriology. 8th ed. Baltimore: Williams & Wilkins; 1974.

Chapter or Selection from an Edited Work

6. Kleiman DG, Brady CA. Coyote behavior in the context of recent canid research: problems and perspectives. In: Bekoff M. editor. Coyotes: biology, behavior, and management. New York: Academic Pr; 1978. pp. 163-88.

Government Document

7. Mech D. The wolves of Isle Royal. National Parks fauna series. Available from: United States GPO, Washington; 1966.

Periodicals

Journal Article by One Author

8. Schenkel R. Expression studies of wolves. Behavior 1947; 1:81-129.

Journal Article by Two or More Authors

9. Sargeant AB, Allen SH. Observed interactions between coyotes and red foxes. J. Mamm. 1989; 70:631-3.

Article with No Identified Author

10. Anonymous. Frustrated hamsters run on their wheels. Nat. Sci. 1981; 91:407.

Newspaper Article

11. Rensberger B, Specter B. CFCs may be destroyed by natural process. Washington Post 1989 Aug 7; Sect 1A: 2 (col 5).

Magazine Article

12. Aveni AF. Emissaries to the stars: the astronomers of ancient Maya.

    Mercury 1995 May: 15-8.

Electronic Media Internet formats are covered briefly in *Scientific Style and Format: The CBE Manual for Authors, Editors, and Publishers,* 6th ed. The CSE Website refers users to the following publication: "National Library of Medicine Recommended Formats for Bibliographic Citation," which expands basic CBE citation conventions to encompass electronic journals and print-based Internet sources.

WEBLINK

http://www.nlm.nih.gov/
pubs/formats/internet.pdf

A Web document
summarizing this style

Online Professional or Personal Site

13. Gelt J. Home use of greywater: rainwater conserves water--and money

    [Internet]. 1993 [cited 1996 Nov 8]. Available from:

    http://www.ag.arizona.edu/AZWATER/arroyo/071.rain.html

Online Book

14. Merck. The Merck index on-line [monograph on the Internet]. 10th ed.

    Rahway (NJ): Merck; 1972 [cited 1990 Dec 7]. Available from:

    http://www.merck.com/pubs

Article in an Online Periodical

15. Lechner DE, Bradbury SF, Bradley LA. Phys Ther J [serial on the

    Internet]. 1998 Aug [cited 1998 Sept 15]. Available from:

    http://www.apta.org/pt_journal/Aug98/Toc.htm

PART 3

Design, Web Sites, and
Special Communications

CHAPTER **7**

Design in Print and on the Web

In today's consumer-oriented, message-dense society, people are inundated with advertisements, solicitations, entertainment, news reports, and all other manner of electronic and print documents. In this environment, people tend to read selectively, focusing only on documents that are interesting, inviting, and clear.

WEBLINK

www.impressiveprinters
.com/

Click on "Ideas" and
explore!

This is where *document design* comes in. By using headings, itemized lists, graphics, white space, effective layouts, and special typefaces, you can increase the chances that people will read your writing. These design elements also can help you emphasize the most important parts of your writing.

7a Follow the three basic design principles

Adhering to the three basic principles of graphic design will make your documents more meaningful and more readable. These principles, which we will refer to as "the three C's," are clustering, contrasting, and connecting.

1 Clustering: grouping closely related items

Ideas or concepts that are closely related in meaning or communicative value should be clustered together visually. Instead of listing these similar concepts separately, consider how you can group them on the page for greater visual impact.

2 Contrasting: highlighting differences

A second way of using design to make documents more meaningful and readable is to create visual contrasts that mirror important differences in content. Using variety in type size and font makes it immediately clear to the reader that elements of a document differ in content and purpose.

3 Connecting: relating every part to some other part

The third way of employing design to make text more coherent is to repeat important graphical or typographical elements—that is, visually connect different parts of a document so that no single element is left stranded. These connections should not be made haphazardly but, rather, in a way that underscores connections in meaning, value, or purpose.

7b   Use formatting tools

Formatting is another powerful way of using visual representation to make a document easier to read and more emphatic in its message. Formatting can be done for decorative reasons only, but it is more effective if it also helps readers understand the text. Today's word-processing programs provide all the formatting tools you are likely to need, from boldface type to hanging indents.

1 Headings

Headings (and subheadings and titles) draw attention, mark off parts of a text, and give the reader a quick sense of what those parts are about. Headings are especially beneficial for readers who only skim a text instead of reading it closely. Headings should give the reader an idea of what the paper, section, or illustration is about. They should be no longer than four or five words.

2 Itemized lists

Itemized lists are a powerful form of visual clustering, as they show how several things form a closely related set. There are two main types of list formats. A *numbered list* or *lettered list* has ordered numbers or letters, suggesting either a ranking of the items or a stepwise procedure. A *bulleted list*, which uses bullets (•), diamonds (♦), dashes (—), or some other symbol, is useful for an unordered set of items.

3 Indentation and spacing

In academic papers, the first line of each paragraph is customarily indented five spaces or $\frac{1}{2}$ inch. With a word processor, you can set this indentation automatically, using either the ruler or the PARAGRAPH feature on the FORMAT menu. Quotations longer than four lines of prose or three lines of poetry are set off as a block, with each line indented ten spaces (see 20d-2).

4 Margins

For academic papers, the standard margin is 1 inch all around, to give the instructor space in which to write comments. These are also the default margins used by most word-processing programs. Word processors are normally set to *left-justify* your text—that is, start lines at the left margin and leave the right margin ragged, thus avoiding the need to hyphenate at the end of a line. Academic papers are usually written with left justification.

5 Frames and boxes

An effective way to highlight a paragraph, graphic, or other part of a document is by putting a rectangular frame or box around it. Frames and boxes are especially useful for summarizing main points or procedural steps, because they simultaneously cluster these points or steps and set them off, through contrast, from the rest of the text.

6 Columns

Putting text into columns is a useful way of clustering information in documents such as brochures, newsletters, résumés, and Web pages. There are basically two kinds of columns: newspaper and tabular. In *newspaper columns*, the text starts on the left, flows down the first column, and then continues at the top of the next column to the right. Newspaper columns are created with the COLUMNS feature on the FORMAT menu. *Tabular columns* consist of independent texts side by side; they are created by using the TABLE feature on a word processor.

7 Typography

Typography refers to all the features associated with individual letters, numbers, and other symbols: font type, font style, font size, color, and case.

Font type refers to the distinctive design of the typeface; some of the most common font types are `Courier,` Times New Roman, Garamond, and Arial. Font types that have little extra lines (*serifs*) at the ends of the letter strokes are called *serif fonts*. *Sans serif* (literally, "without serif") *fonts* lack such extra lines.

Font style (or *font weight*) refers to the particular variant of a single typeface: regular, *italic*, **bold**, or ***bold italic***. Italic, bold, and bold italic typefaces can all be used for emphasis, but they have other uses as well.

The standard *font size* range for academic papers is 10 to 12 points, with section headings often set in 14-point type and the title of the paper in 20- or even 24-point type. More specialized bulletins or reports may use a wider range of heading sizes and styles.

Color is another option that has become available with the widespread use of computers. Like bold and italic type, however, color should be used sparingly—and systematically.

One other typographical variable is *case*. Academic writers normally use the standard combination of lowercase (small) and uppercase (capital) letters, except for acronyms and other abbreviations.

8 Page numbering

In a multipage document, it is a good idea to number the pages. Consult your word processor's documentation on how to operate the PAGE NUMBERING feature.

7c Use graphics

Graphics include tables, line graphs, bar graphs, pie charts, clip art, photographs, cartoons, drawings, maps, and other forms of visual art.

1 Tables

Tables are the best type of graphic for presenting a lot of data in compressed form. Current word-processing programs offer a variety of table formats to choose from. Just click on TABLE and explore the options your program gives you.

2 Line graphs

Line graphs generally do not contain as much data as tables do. But they can make data more understandable and are especially effective for showing changes over time. If a graph has more than one line, be sure to distinguish the various lines clearly (for example, by having one solid, another dotted, and a third dashed). Do not use more than three lines in a graph, as too many lines will produce a cluttered effect.

3 Bar graphs

Bar graphs emphasize discrete points rather than continuity, but they can also show changes over time, sometimes more dramatically than line graphs.

WEBLINK

http://writing.colostate.edu/
references/graphics.cfm

An excellent guide to using illustrations, graphics, tables, and figures in document design

4 Pie charts

Pie charts are effective in showing how a fixed quantity of something is divided into fractions. Generally, the entire "pie" should represent 100 percent.

5 Clip art

Clip art, or ready-made images, can add a decorative touch to a document. Do not get carried away, though; too much of a good thing may only distract or annoy readers. Be especially cautious about using clip art in academic papers.

WEBLINK

http://www.clip-art.com

A great list of links to free graphics, icons, and other stuff on the Web

6 Photographs, cartoons, drawings, and maps

The advent of graphical scanners and Internet downloading has made it easy to incorporate photographs and other images (such as cartoons, drawings, and maps) into documents. But remember that you cannot use copyrighted materials, such as cartoons or photographs created by someone else, without that person's permission.

7d   Designing for the Web: Generate a basic design

Writing for the Web is not all that different from writing for other purposes. The basic principles outlined in Part 1 of this handbook still apply. Web documents differ from print documents in two important ways: they tend to include more graphics than print documents do, and they are hypertextual (that is, they have electronic links).

> **WEBLINK**
>
> http://www.w3.org/Provider/
> Style/Introduction.html
> A hypertextually organized
> manual on Web design from
> the creator of the www,
> Tim Berners-Lee

When a Web page is well designed, the author's message is successfully conveyed to readers, and the look and content of the page match the purposes of the author. Thus, effectively designed Web sites make good use of both graphics and hypertext.

1 Using graphics effectively

In print media, the printed words convey most of the text's meaning. But even printed texts contain other meaningful visual cues in addition to the words themselves—for example, by using boldface type for chapter titles, we also convey meaning. When Web authors consider document design, formatting, and graphics, they make decisions similar to those made by writers of print documents. However, the role of visual features in conveying meaning is greater in Web documents than in print documents.

2 Using hypertext effectively

Hypertext goes a logical step beyond print by allowing busy readers to choose among short chunks of text on specific topics, deciding what to read and what to ignore. Hypertext is text that is broken down into discrete pieces, which are then connected through electronic links.

3 Basic design elements

As you think about your Web site, you will need to consider whether to use some basic design elements to structure the Web pages, such as tables, frames, style sheets, and Javascript. Depending on your site's purpose and the needs of your audience, you can select among these design options.

Using Tables Tables are used by Web page authors to control page layout so that text and graphics appear on the page where they'd like them to appear. When using tables, you can decide on the number of columns and rows that will be used on each page and what data will "fill" cells formed by the intersection of those columns and rows.

Using Frames Frames are used in a similar way as tables to organize the text and graphics on a Web site. They differ from tables, though, in their ability to show in the browser window multiple files displayed in different portions of the frame. The frame itself consistently appears on the page, but different Web pages may be displayed within the frame windows.

Using Style Sheets Style sheets provide another sophisticated way to format your Web pages. Style sheets for the Web work in much the same way as style sheets for word-processing programs. They allow you to set default elements such as fonts and colors that will then be applied uniformly to your document.

Using Javascript Javascript is a programming language that allows for miniature programs to be embedded into Web pages as *applets*. These applets can perform functions within a larger Web page, generating information that would otherwise have been sent over the Internet. Javascript is a complicated language to learn and beyond the scope of this book. However, if you would like to learn more on your own, you can go to Sun Microsystem's Web site (http://www. javasoft.com).

7e Methods used to construct Web pages

Once you have an overall plan for your Web site, you can begin to compose your Web pages. The text of a Web site—what it "says" to the reader—is as important as how it looks; Web pages communicate through both text and graphics.

There are several methods by which to compose your Web pages—or you may use a combination of these methods:

1 Use an HTML editor or composer, software that is designed to help with writing Web pages.

Some commonly used commercial HTML editors include *Macromedia Dreamweaver, Adobe PageMill, Microsoft Front Page*, or *Claris Home Page*. There are also HTML editors available in freeware versions that can be downloaded from the Internet (e.g., *HomeSite*). The most popular Internet browsers, *Netscape* and *Explorer*, also include their own HTML editor/composers, along with useful advice and tutorials on writing Web pages.

2 Use a translator program that changes a word-processing or database file into a Web file.

Newer versions of *Microsoft Word, WordPerfect, Excel*, and *PowerPoint*, for example, all include a SAVE AS HTML command, typically found in the FILE, SAVE AS menu. You choose this option when you have already written an extensive text in a word-processing program that you want to convert into a Web file.

3 Use a text-editing or word-processing program (e.g., *Windows NotePad* or *Microsoft Word*) and enter the HTML code by hand.

This is the most difficult and time-consuming method for composing Web pages. However, despite the help of the sophisticated editors and composers available today, sometimes it is still necessary to insert HTML codes by hand in order to achieve exactly the result you desire.

7f HTML editors and HTML codes

HyperText Markup Language (HTML) is not really a language but rather a system for embedding codes into text. These codes tell a Web browser how to display the text in the browser window. To introduce yourself to HTML, surf the Web until you find a site that you think is lively and well designed. View the source code of the site by selecting VIEW HTML SOURCE or VIEW PAGE SOURCE on most browsers.

There are three methods currently used to generate HTML files: (1) using an HTML editor or composer, (2) using a translator program to save a word-processed document as an HTML file, or (3) embedding the HTML code by hand. Most Web authors begin with either method (1) or (2), but also find that they need to embed some codes by hand. There are many good reference books that can teach you the details of HTML coding.

7g   Refine your Web site

Once you have created your homepage and secondary pages, review them carefully to ensure that the text is correct, the links are accurate, the graphics are well located, and the overall look of the site is pleasing. Refine your Web site, using the HTML editor of your choice. Preview your pages in the browser window from time to time to see how the site is shaping up.

1 Checking the text

Web texts should be written in simple, direct sentences that speak to all visitors to the site. You should typically use the second person "you" when addressing your readers. Since many readers may enter your site via secondary pages rather than the homepage, make certain that the text on each page is explanatory enough to stand on its own.

2 Checking the relative and remote links

The relative links—to other Web pages on the same site and to other destinations on the same Web page—should all work in the browser window. If they do not, go back to the editing HTML sources window and check your codes. Internet browsers are extremely literal—if a period or a quotation mark is missing in the code, the link will not work.

The remote links—to Web sites other than your own—should all be checked with the Internet browser. Open each page in the browser to ensure that all of the links connect you to the correct location on the Web. If they do not, you need to go back to the HTML editing window to check our codes. The URL for the link must be typed *exactly* as it is listed at the site or the link will not work.

3 Checking the graphics

When you open your document in the Internet browser, the graphics that you have included should all appear. To check, open your Web pages in both major browsers, *Explorer* and *Netscape*, because browsers can differ as to how they display the pages and the graphics.

4 Checking the overall look

As a final check, open your Web site in your Internet browser (using the OPEN FILE IN BROWSER option from the FILE menu). Try to read the site as an objective reader might. Do you think your message will come across to your intended audience?

7h   Transfer your site to an Internet server

Prior to sending the Web files to your Internet server, be certain that your site is exactly as you want it to be. Once the files are on the server, they will stay there until you send them again. You cannot edit your Web site from the server. Rather, you have to edit the files in the HTML editor and transfer them again, overwriting the original files. Use FTP (file transfer protocol) or PUBLISHER to send your Web files to the Internet server.

CHAPTER **8**

Writing for Different Purposes

In college and on the job, much of the writing you do will be "on demand"—that is, you will have a limited time in which to complete it. In college, such writing often takes the form of a timed essay exam or an in-class writing assignment. In the workplace, you may be writing a letter or an email document, or even preparing an oral presentation. Each of these different formats requires some adjustment of your writing style.

8a   Write concise and professional business letters

Business letters typically are addressed to a specific person, but they may be circulated to other readers as well. Thus, you should make the purpose of your letter clear at the outset, and you should anticipate the possibility that someone other than the addressee (an assistant, for example) might read it. Be sure to provide whatever background information these readers might need. Be clear and concise (see Chapter 15), and try to strike a friendly, courteous, and professional tone (see 17c).

WEBLINK

http://writing.colostate.edu/
references/documents/bletter

A great guide to writing
business letters

8b   Write specifically tailored letters of application

A letter of application has the same general format as a business letter. It should be brief (no more than one page). The first paragraph should state clearly what position you are applying for. The next paragraph or two should describe your primary credentials for the position. The closing paragraph should express your desire for an interview and give the reader information about your availability.

8c   Write appropriately packed résumés

A résumé is a concise summary of an individual's accomplishments, skills, experience, and personal interests. It is more complete and inclusive than a letter of application.

A résumé should be densely packed with appropriate information. Most résumés use five standard categories of information: (1) Position Desired or Objective, (2) Education, (3) Experience or Employment, (4) Related Activities, and (5) References, in that order.

1 Formatting a traditional résumé

A traditional résumé should be pleasing to the eye. Use suitable margins (about 1 inch all around), and use white space to set off the major categories and groupings. Use boldface type for your name and for major headings and subheadings. Using active-voice verbs will give you a dynamic image.

2 Formatting a scannable résumé

Many companies are now using computer technology to create résumé databanks that can be computer-scanned for keywords. Take advantage of this technology by putting keyword self-descriptors such as *retail sales* and *management experience* in a separate section at the beginning of your résumé.

Computer scanners are not always reliable when it comes to distinguishing letters, numbers, and other marks on paper, so avoid anything fancy. Start every line at the left margin; do not use columns. Use light-colored, standard-size paper, a conventional typeface, and 10- to 14-point font sizes. Do not use italics, underlining, color, lines, graphics, or boxes. Print out the résumé on a high-quality printer. Do not fold or staple the résumé.

3 Formatting an electronic résumé

Many companies solicit résumés via email or the Internet. In such cases, you should format your résumé so that it conforms to the company's specifications. This usually means (1) using a simplified layout with a prominent keywords section, like that of the scannable résumé discussed above, and (2) putting the document in ASCII, Text Only, or Simple Text format. Rather than sending the résumé as an attached file, most companies prefer that you embed it in the email message you send in response to the company's solicitation, placing the résumé after the cover letter.

8d   Practice good email etiquette

WEBLINK

http://www.albion.com/
netiquette/

A great netiquette
homepage

Electronic mail (email) is now widely used in most corporate and academic settings. Learning the special rules of the Internet, nicknamed *netiquette*, enables you to use this medium to best effect.

Behaviors that are not acceptable in other settings, such as verbal or sexual harassment, will not be tolerated on the

Internet. Additionally, it is not appropriate to use your classmates' or employer's email addresses for chain letters, advertising, or other similar purposes. Nor is it appropriate to use those addresses to ask someone out on a date. Also, be sensitive about "flaming"—writing angry or abusive messages. If you are flamed, do not reply in kind. Either ignore the message or respond calmly.

8e　Use file attachments

Many email systems allow you to attach files or documents to your messages. Check your mailing system for an ATTACHMENT option. Using attachments is a convenient way to send your work to a classmate for peer review or to an employer if you are away from the office. One of the advantages of using attachments over the copy-and-paste method of incorporating text into an email message is that much of your word-processing format can be preserved.

8f　Use instant messaging

Another feature of email communication is called *instant messaging,* which allows you to create a circle of email friends, classmates, or colleagues who are also users of the same network (e.g., *AOL* or *MSN*). The instant messaging service will notify you whenever someone on your email group list is also online so that you can begin a "chat" session with that person via the network, should you desire to do so. (You will not be added to someone's instant messaging circle without your prior approval.)

8g　Prepare thoroughly for oral presentations

In many careers, the ability to communicate orally is just as important as the ability to write well. The basic principle to keep in mind in preparing any kind of oral presentation is this: *all listeners have a limited attention span;* thus, you cannot expect them to follow closely everything you say. Their attention will probably wander from time to time, even if your presentation is only ten minutes long. So, if you want to make sure your listeners will come away from your talk with your main points clear in their minds, you must organize your presentation in such a way that these main points stand out:

1. *Limit your topic to what your audience needs to know;* don't digress.
2. *Select effective supporting information,* either data or evidence that will support your main point.
3. *Choose an appropriate organization* for your material, just as you would for a written paper.
4. *Prepare an outline,* including the main points and main supporting points only.
5. *Select appropriate visual aids.*
6. *Prepare a suitable introduction,* so that your audience will be interested in what you have to say.
7. *Prepare a closing summary,* and re-emphasize your main points.

8h   Pick your visual aids carefully

Visual aids are of great help in giving an oral presentation. First, they serve as "cue cards," reminding you of all your important points and allowing you to stay on track without reading from a manuscript or from notes. Second, visual aids have tremendous power as attention-getters. Studies have shown that people remember the visual parts of speeches far better than they do the verbal parts. Finally, visual aids can help clarify your message.

Pick your visual aids carefully. Here are the basic options:

- *PowerPoint* projection
- Overhead transparencies
- Chalkboard
- Flip charts or posters
- Handouts
- 3-dimensional objects

Each of these technologies has its own strengths and weaknesses, and should be evaluated with the following questions in mind: Is it easy to prepare? Can it be altered easily during the presentation? Will it allow you to control the audience's attention—or will it distract attention from what you're saying? Will it let you present at an appropriate speed? How much information can it convey? How large an audience can you use it with? How reliable is it—does it depend on electronic equipment? Can the audience keep it for future reference? How well does it work as a "cue card"?

8i Practice, practice, practice

Nothing is more helpful to the ultimate success of an oral presentation than practice. Not even the best of speakers can give a totally effective presentation without first practicing it. Practice allows you to spot the flaws in a presentation and correct them. It enables you to work on making smooth transitions instead of awkward stops and starts. Practice gives you an idea of how long your presentation will take, allowing you to make adjustments so that you can ultimately deliver it at a comfortable tempo. All of these benefits promote greater self-confidence, which will give you a more emphatic, convincing, and effective style of delivery.

8j Use *PowerPoint*

Presentation software such as *PowerPoint* is becoming more and more common because it has almost all the benefits of overhead transparencies plus some special advantages: it projects color better than overhead transparencies; it can include animation, video, and sound; and it can be converted into HTML and put on a Web site for later reference. Also, it has a wizard and templates to guide you through the process of putting together a presentation. Although the templates are business-oriented, some of them can be adapted to academic presentations as well.

As with overhead transparencies, *PowerPoint* slides should be neatly formatted, easily readable, and not too cluttered with information. If the presentation is in a darkened room, the slides should have a light background; in a well-lit room, they should have a darker background. Any visual images or background sound should be relevant to the theme of the presentation.

> **WEBLINK**
>
> http://www.ruf.rice.edu/
> ~riceowl/oralpres.html
> "Designing Effective Oral Presentations." Good step-by-step advice from the Rice University Online Writing Lab
>
> http://www.canberra.edu.au/studyskills/learning/oralpres.html
> Helpful tips for preparing and delivering an oral presentation, with advice on the use of *PowerPoint*

CHAPTER 9

Sentence Structure

Improving your grammar and writing style will allow you to express your thoughts more precisely and make your writing more readable and interesting. To improve your style, you will need to know the basic elements of sentence structure. This chapter provides that information.

9a Learn to identify parts of speech

In writing a sentence, you put words together in certain combinations. These combinations depend, in part, on the different kinds of words, or parts of speech, you use: nouns, pronouns, verbs, adjectives, adverbs, prepositions, conjunctions, and interjections.

1 Nouns

A **noun** (n) is the name of a person, place, thing, quality, idea, or action. Some examples of nouns are

Picasso	Mexico	printer
honesty	democracy	stamp collecting

Nouns are often preceded by *a, an,* or *the;* these words are known as *articles.* Use *a* before nouns beginning with consonant sounds; use *an* before nouns beginning with vowel sounds: *a* printer, *an* insult.

Common nouns refer to general persons, places, things, concepts, or qualities: *city, generosity*.

Proper nouns, which are almost always capitalized, name particular persons, places, institutions, organizations, months, and days: *Buddhism, Monday*.

Concrete nouns specifically refer to things that can be sensed through sight, hearing, touch, taste, or smell: *bookshelf, thunder*.

Abstract nouns refer to ideas, emotions, qualities, or other intangible concepts: *sadness, truth*.

Count nouns name things that can be counted and thus can have a plural form: *violin(s), goose (geese)*.

Noncount nouns, or mass nouns, name things that typically are not counted in English and thus cannot be made plural: *water, health*.

Collective nouns name groups; they are plural in sense but singular in form: *committee, crowd*.

2 Pronouns

Pronouns (pron), such as *she, they,* and *it,* are words that substitute for nouns. The noun a pronoun substitutes for is called the **antecedent** of the pronoun. The noun antecedent often precedes the pronoun in a sentence:

Lucinda said *she* was not feeling well.

Sometimes the noun antedecent follows the pronoun:

Saying *she* was not feeling well, *Lucinda* left the room.

Pronouns can be singular or plural, and their case form can vary depending on how they are used in a sentence. (See Chapter 10 for a discussion of pronoun case and pronoun-antecedent agreement.)

3 Verbs

A **verb** (v) is a word that expresses an action (*swim, read*) or a state of being (*is, seemed*). Main verbs are often accompanied by **auxiliary verbs** (also called helping verbs), which include forms of the verbs *be, have,* and *do,* and/or by *modal verbs,* such as *may, might, can, could, will, would, shall, should,* and *must*. Auxiliary and modal verbs are critical parts of special verb forms that express questions, future tenses, past tenses, and various degrees of doubt about or qualification of the main verb's action. (See Chapter 10 for more on verbs.)

Transitive verbs (vt) transfer action from an agent (usually the subject of the sentence) to an object or recipient (usually the direct object of the sentence): "Michael *fumbled* the ball." **Intransitive verbs** (vi) may express action, but they do not transfer it to an object or recipient: "The bridge *collapsed*."

Verbs also have an active form, called the **active voice** ("He *committed* the crime"), as well as a passive form, called the **passive voice**, consisting of a form of the verb *be* and a past participle ("The crime *was committed* by him"). Verbs may take alternative forms for different **moods.** In the **indicative mood,** they make assertions, state opinions, and ask questions. Past-tense forms express unreal conditions or wishes, in the **subjunctive mood:** "I wish I *were* in Hawaii." They appear in the base form to issue a command, in the **imperative mood:** "Don't *do* that again!" or, occasionally, "Don't you *do* that again!"

4 Verbals

A **verbal** is a verb form that functions in a sentence as a noun, an adverb, or an adjective. There are three types of verbals: participles, gerunds, and infinitives.

Participles are words such as *sweeping* and *swept*, the present and past participles of a verb (*sweep*) that function as adjectives and can modify nouns or pronouns: "Beware of *sweeping* generalizations." "Keep floors *swept*."

Gerunds are verb forms that end in *ing* and function as nouns: "*Sweeping* is something I do not enjoy."

An **infinitive** is the base form of a verb, often preceded by *to* (*to read, to fly*). Infinitives can function as nouns, adjectives, or adverbs: "To quit would be a mistake." "Her desire *to quit* is understandable."

5 Adjectives

An **adjective** (adj) is a word that modifies a noun or pronoun by qualifying or describing it. In English, the adjective usually precedes the noun it modifies (an *old* tree, the *other* day). In sentences such as "The program was *challenging*," the adjective falls on the other side of a verb linking it to the noun it modifies. An adjective used in this way is called a **predicate adjective.**

Many adjectives have comparative and superlative forms created by the addition of -*er* and -*est* (*small, smaller, smallest*). (See Chapter 10.) Many other adjectives have the same form as the present or past participle of a verb (a *roaring* lion, a *deserted* island).

6 Adverbs

An **adverb** (adv) modifies a verb, an adjective, another adverb, or an entire clause or sentence. Adverbs usually answer one of the following questions: when? where? how? how often? to what extent?

> The mayor lives *alone* in a downtown apartment.   [*Alone* modifies the verb *lives.*]

> She has a *very* busy schedule.   [*Very* modifies the adjective *busy.*]

Conjunctive adverbs, such as *however, thus,* and *consequently,* modify an entire sentence or clause while linking it to the preceding sentence or clause. (See Chapter 10.)

7 Prepositions

A **preposition** (prep) is a word such as *in, on, of, for,* or *by* that comes before a noun or pronoun and its modifiers to form a **prepositional phrase** (*in the water, off the deep end*). The noun or pronoun in such phrases (*water, end, them*) is called the **object of the preposition.** Prepositions also occur in multiword combinations: *according to, along with, because of,* and *with respect to.* Prepositions can be linked to certain verbs to form **phrasal verbs,** such as *do without, put up with,* and *look over.* In phrasal verbs, the preposition is called a **particle.**

8 Conjunctions

A **conjunction** (conj) joins two sentences, clauses, phrases, or words. The relationship between the two parts may be an equal, or coordinate, one; it may be an unequal, or subordinate, one.

Coordinating conjunctions (*and, but, or, nor, yet, so, for*) connect sentences, clauses, phrases, or words that are parallel in meaning and grammatical structure. **Correlative conjunctions** (*both/and, neither/nor, either/or, not/but,* *whether/or, not only/but also*) are pairs of conjunctions that give extra emphasis to the two parts of a coordinated construction. **Subordinating conjunctions** introduce dependent clauses and connect them to main clauses. Some common subordinating conjunctions are *although, because, if, since, unless,* and *while.*

9 Interjections

An interjection is a short utterance like *wow!* or *ouch!* that expresses an emotional response. Interjections usually stand alone and are punctuated with an exclamation mark.

9b   Learn to identify basic sentence patterns

Sentences are the basic units for expressing assertions, questions, commands, wishes, and exclamations. All grammatically complete sentences have a subject and a predicate. In a sentence fragment, one of these elements may be missing. (See Chapter 11 for more on fragments.)

1 Sentence subjects

The **subject** (sub) of a sentence is a noun, a pronoun, or a noun phrase that identifies what the sentence is about. Usually it directly precedes the main verb.

> *You* probably have a pointing device (PD) connected to your computer.
> *Many PDs* have a ball that rolls against wheels.

The **simple subject** is always a noun or pronoun. In the example sentence, the simple subject is *you*. The complete subject is the simple subject plus all its modifiers; the complete subjects are italicized in the example sentences. Some sentences have a **compound subject** including two or more simple subjects: "*Tips and techniques* can be found in the HELP menu." In imperative sentences, which express a command or a request, the subject is understood to be *you*, even though it is not usually stated: "[You] Wake up!" The subject of a sentence always agrees in number with the main verb. That is, a singular subject takes a singular verb, and a plural subject takes a plural verb: "Many PDs . . . have." Subject-verb agreement is discussed further in Chapter 12.

2 Predicates

The **predicate** is the part of a sentence that contains the verb and makes a statement about the subject. The **simple predicate** is the verb plus any auxiliary (helping) verbs: "With a Web browser, you *can locate* information efficiently." The **complete predicate** consists of the simple predicate plus any objects, complements, or adverbial modifiers: "The World Wide Web *offers information, media, and software.*" A **compound predicate** has two or more verbs that have the same subject: "A Web page *informs and entertains.*"

A **direct object** (DO) is a noun, a pronoun, or a noun phrase that completes the action of a transitive verb (see 9b-3)—one that is capable of transmitting action. In this sentence, *information* is the direct object of the verb *locate*:

Sub   V   DO
You can locate *information*.

An **indirect object** (IO) is a noun, a pronoun, or a noun phrase that is affected indirectly by the action of a verb. It usually refers to the recipient or beneficiary of the action described by the verb and the direct object.

Sub   V   IO   DO
The teacher told *us* a story.

Most indirect objects can be presented instead as the object of the preposition *to* or *for*:

The teacher told *us* a story.   OR   The teacher told a story *to us*.

An **object complement** (OC) is a noun, a noun phrase, an adjective, or an adjective phrase that elaborates on or describes the direct object.

Sub   V   DO   OC
The news made us *depressed*.

A **subject complement** (SC) is a noun, a noun phrase, an adjective, or an adjective phrase that follows a linking verb (such as *is, was,* or *seems*) and elaborates on the subject:

```
Sub  LV  SC   Sub LV              SC
```
Laurie is *happy*. She is *the new head of the task force.*

3 Basic sentence patterns

The complete predicate is usually structured according to one of five basic sentence patterns:

Pattern 1: A sentence may have an intransitive verb and no object.

```
       Pred
Sub     V
```
Time flies.

Pattern 2: A sentence may have a transitive verb with a direct object.

```
           Pred
Sub   VT        DO
```
Time heals all wounds.

Pattern 3: A sentence may have a transitive verb with a direct object and an indirect object.

```
              Pred
Sub     VT  IO       DO
```
Free time gave us an opportunity.

Pattern 4: A sentence may have a transitive verb with a direct object and an object complement.

```
              Pred
Sub     VT  DO  OC
```
Time pressures made us tense.

Pattern 5: A sentence may use a **linking verb,** which connects the subject to a subject complement, indicating a condition, quality, or state of being.

```
        Pred
      ┌──────────┐
Sub   LV  SC
```

Time is precious.

9c Learn to expand sentences

The five basic sentence patterns can be expanded using words, phrases, or clauses to modify the subject or predicate.

1 Modifying with single words

Any simple sentence part can be modified, qualified, or described by appropriate single words. Verbs, adverbs, and adjectives can be modified by adverbs, and nouns can be modified by adjectives: "Time flies *quickly*." "*Spare* time flies *very quickly*." See Chapter 10 for more on placing adjectives and adverbs.

2 Modifying with phrases

Sentence parts can also be modified by phrases. A **phrase** is a group of words consisting of (1) a noun and its related words or (2) a verbal and its related words. Phrases add detail to any of the subjects, verbs, objects, or complements used in the five basic sentence patterns.

Adding Prepositional Phrases A preposition and its object (a noun or pronoun) form a prepositional phrase: *in the dark, on time, outside Dallas.* Prepositional phrases can be used to modify nouns, verbs, or adjectives.

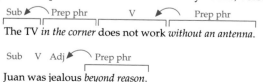

Adding Verbal Phrases   A verbal is a verb form that functions as a noun, an adverb, or an adjective (see 9a-4). The three kinds of verbals—infinitives, gerunds, and participles—can be combined with other words to form infinitive phrases, gerund phrases, and participial phrases.

An **infinitive phrase** consists of the base form of a verb (sometimes preceded by *to*) plus modifiers, objects, and/or complements. Such a phrase can function as a noun, an adjective, or an adverb.

> We wanted *to plant the garden*. [Infinitive phrase as a noun]
>
> This gave us a chance *to reflect*. [Infinitive phrase as an adjective]
>
> The company was eager *to expand*. [Infinitive phrase as an adverb]

A **gerund phrase** consists of the *-ing* form of a verb plus modifiers, objects, and/or complements. Gerund phrases function as nouns and thus can be used as sentence subjects, objects, or complements.

> Sub
> _____
> *Lifting boxes all day* made Stan tired.

A **participial phrase** consists of a present participle (the *-ing* form of a verb) or a past participle (the *-ed* or *-en* form of a verb) plus modifiers, objects, and/or complements. Participial phrases function as adjectives, modifying subjects and objects of sentences. (See Chapter 13.)

> *Having decided to quit his job*, Roberto began looking for another one.
> [The participial phrase modifies the sentence subject, *Roberto*.]

Adding Appositive Phrases   An **appositive phrase** is a noun phrase that describes or defines another noun. Appositive phrases directly follow or precede the nouns they modify and are usually set off by commas.

> The Ford Mustang, *a car originally designed by Lee Iacocca*, has been an enduring icon of the US automotive industry.

Adding Absolute Phrases   An **absolute phrase** consists of a subject and an adjective phrase (most commonly a participial phrase). Unlike other kinds of phrases, which can modify single words, absolute phrases are used to modify entire clauses or sentences.

> *His curiosity fully satisfied*, Marco decided to move on to other topics.

3 Modifying with clauses

A **clause** is a group of words that has a subject and a predicate. If a clause can stand alone as a sentence, it is an **independent clause** (or main clause); if it cannot, it is a **dependent clause** (or *subordinate clause*). There are three major types of dependent clauses: adjective, adverb, and noun.

Adjective clauses (also called relative clauses) modify nouns and pronouns. An adjective clause usually begins with a relative pronoun (*which, that, who, whose, whom*) or a subordinating conjunction (*where, when, how*) and immediately follows the noun or pronoun it modifies.

The student *who is best prepared* is most likely to succeed.

Noun clauses function in a sentence the way simple nouns do—as subjects, objects, complements, or appositives. A noun clause begins with a relative pronoun (*who, that, whom, whoever*) or a subordinate conjunction (*whatever, wherever, how, why*).

Sub

Whoever leaked the news should be punished.

Ob

No one seems to know *how the rumor got started*.

Adverb clauses modify verbs, adjectives, clauses, or other adverbs, answering questions such as the following: when? where? why? how? An adverb clause begins with a subordinating conjunction (*if, although, because, whenever, while*).

If you cannot find the topic you want, double-click on the HELP button.

9d   Learn to classify sentences

Good writers vary the types of sentences they use in order to make their writing more interesting. The two main categories of sentence types are functional and structural.

1 Functional classifications

Sentences can be categorized functionally, or rhetorically, according to their role. A declarative sentence, for example, makes a direct assertion about something: "Our political system is heavily influenced by corporate interests." An **interrogative sentence** asks a question and ends with a question mark: "Have you ever traveled overseas?" An **imperative sentence** makes a request, gives a command, or offers advice. Although it is always addressed to *you*, the pronoun is usually omitted: "Use the TOOLBAR buttons to align or indent text." An exclamatory sentence expresses strong emotion and ends with an exclamation point: "We're finally connected!"

2 Structural classifications

Sentences can also be categorized structurally according to their overall grammatical construction. A **simple sentence** has a single independent clause and no dependent clauses. Although a simple sentence has only one clause, it may have many phrases and thus be quite long.

> I walk.

> The high plateau of western Bolivia, called the *altiplano*, is one of the world's highest-elevation populated regions, with several towns at over 12,000 feet above sea level.

A **compound sentence** has two or more independent clauses and no dependent clauses. A compound sentence is created when two or more independent clauses are connected with a comma and a coordinating conjunction (*and, or, but, nor, for, so, yet*), with a semicolon and a conjunctive adverb (*therefore, however, otherwise, indeed*), with a semicolon alone, or with a correlative conjunction (*either/or, neither/nor, both/and, not only/but also*).

> Ind cl | Ind cl
> An eagle once flew past our house, *but* I got only a brief glimpse of it.

A **complex sentence** contains one independent clause and one or more dependent clauses.

> Dep cl | Ind cl
> Although Alaska is a huge state, it has relatively few people.

A **compound-complex sentence**, as the name implies, consists of two or more independent clauses and one or more dependent clauses.

Dep cl

Millions upon millions of years before civilization had risen upon earth,

Ind cl

the central areas of this tremendous ocean were empty; *and*

Dep cl   Ind cl

where famous islands now exist, nothing rose above the rolling waves.

—James Michener, *Hawaii*

CHAPTER **10**

Pronouns, Verbs, Adjectives, and Adverbs

Now that you have learned to identify different parts of speech, you need to learn how to use them correctly. This chapter will help you to avoid common usage problems with pronouns, verbs, adjectives, and adverbs.

PRONOUNS

Sometimes using pronouns in place of nouns can make writing more concise and readable. But pronouns can be confusing to readers if they are not used correctly.

10a Make pronouns agree in number and gender with their antecedents

A **pronoun** substitutes for a noun (or noun equivalent), which is called the **antecedent** of the pronoun (9a-2). Pronouns and their antecedents must agree in number and gender.

Antecedent   Pronoun

Bad luck can happen to anyone, and *it* can happen at any time.

In this sentence, *bad luck* and *it* are both singular; therefore, they agree in *number*. They also agree in gender because *bad luck* is neuter (neither masculine nor feminine) and *it* can serve as a pronoun for neuter antecedents.

Here are some rules on pronoun-antecedent agreement.

1. *A compound antecedent usually is plural and thus requires a plural pronoun.* A **compound antecedent** is a noun phrase containing two or more terms joined by *and*.

   Mr. and Mrs. Kwan are here for *their* appointment.

2. *With disjunctive antecedents, the pronoun should agree in number and gender with the nearest part.* A **disjunctive an-

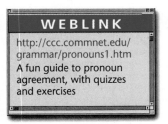

WEBLINK

http://ccc.commnet.edu/
grammar/pronouns1.htm

A fun guide to pronoun
agreement, with quizzes
and exercises

tecedent** is a noun phrase consisting of two or more terms joined by *or* or *nor*. When a disjunctive antecedent contains both a singular and a plural part, this rule works well if the singular noun precedes the plural one.

   Either Tamara Wilson or *the Changs* will bring *their* barbeque set to the next picnic.

If the plural noun precedes the singular one, however, following the rule usually leads to an awkward-sounding sentence:

   Either the Changs or *Tamara Wilson* will bring *her* barbeque set to the next picnic.

In such cases, it is best to reword the sentence so as to either get rid of the pronoun or put the singular noun before the plural one.

3. *As an antecedent, a collective noun can be either singular or plural, depending on its sense.* Both of these sentences are correct:

The jury took only two hours to reach *its* verdict.

The jury took only two hours to reach *their* verdict.

The first sentence emphasizes the singularity of the jury as a body, while the second puts more emphasis on the jury as a group of individuals.

4. *Pronouns must agree with antecedents that are indefinite pronouns.* Most indefinite pronouns (such as *everyday, anyone,* and *each*) are singular. When an indefinite pronoun serves as the antecedent for another pronoun, that pronoun should also be singular.

Everything was in *its* place.

Each of the women had *her* reasons for opposing the plan.

Some indefinite pronouns (*some, all, more*) can have either a singular or a plural sense. When one of these indefinite pronouns is used as the antecedent for another pronoun, the other pronoun can be either singular or plural, depending on the sense of the sentence.

Some of the *news* was as a bad as we thought *it* would be.

Some of the team's *players* have lost *their* motivation.

5. *Sexist use of generic pronouns should be avoided.* In the past, the male pronouns *he, him,* and *his* were often used in generic statements referring to both sexes, as in this sentence: "A doctor should listen carefully to *his* patients." But this practice is clearly sexist, as it favors one gender over the other. Three ways to avoid such sexist pronoun usage are (1) making the pronoun and its antecedent plural, (2) rewording the sentence, and (3) using an occasional disjunctive pronoun such as *he or she*.

10b Refer to a specific noun antecedent

Pronouns (such as *she, it,* and *his*) work best when they refer back to a particular noun (the antecedent).

Only one of the new hockey players knew what *his* position would be.

1 Avoiding generalized *they* or *you* or implied antecedents

In casual speech, people often use pronouns in vague ways, without explicit antecedents ("*They* say that television is dulling our brains"). In formal writing, however, such vagueness can sabotage meaning and must be avoided.

VAGUE *THEY* REVISED

> *Some people*
> ~~They~~ say that television is dulling our brains.

Similarly, avoid using the pronoun *you* unless you are addressing the reader directly.

VAGUE *YOU* REVISED

> *One never knows*
> ~~You never know~~ when calamity will strike.

Pronouns should refer back to specific antecedents, not implied ones.

2 Clarifying references with more than one possible antecedent

Writers sometimes get into trouble by using a pronoun that could refer to more than one noun. Usually it is necessary to rewrite the sentence so that the antecedent is named, whether or not it has been mentioned previously in the sentence.

VAGUE REFERENCE REVISED

> *Fred*
> Neither Bill nor Fred knew what ~~he~~ should do.

OR

> *their friend*
> Neither Bill nor Fred knew what ~~he~~ should do.

If *he* refers either to Fred or to a mutual friend mentioned in a previous sentence, it is important to say so.

10c Avoid vague use of *this, that, which,* and *it*

The pronouns *this, that, which,* and *it* may be used with care to refer broadly to an entire statement:

> According to the linguistic school currently on top, human beings are all born with a genetic endowment for recognizing and formulating language. *This* must mean that we possess genes for all kinds of information, with strands of special, peculiarly human DNA for the discernment of meaning in syntax.
>
> —Lewis Thomas, *Lives of a Cell*

In this excerpt, the word *this* leading off the second sentence refers clearly to the main clause of the first sentence ("human beings . . . language").

In many cases, though, using pronouns for broad reference may confuse the reader. What does *it* refer to in the following paragraph?

> Watching Monday Night Football on ABC has become a ritual for countless American sports lovers. It is symbolic of contemporary American life.

It could refer to (1) Monday Night Football, (2) watching Monday Night Football, or (3) watching Monday Night Football has become a ritual for countless American sports lovers. One way to resolve this ambiguity is to replace the pronoun with a full noun phrase:

VAGUE REFERENCE REVISED

> Watching Monday Night Football on ABC has become a ritual for
> *Monday Night Football*
> countless American sports lovers. ~~It~~ is symbolic of contemporary
> American life.

10d Be consistent with use of *that* and *which*

The relative pronoun *that* is used only with essential (restrictive) relative clauses—clauses that are essential to identify the nouns they modify:

ESSENTIAL CLAUSE

First prize went to the longhaired collie *that came all the way from Hartford.*
[There were other long-haired collies in the competition.]

Although many people prefer using *which* only for nonessential relative clauses, it can be used either with essential relative clauses or with non-essential (nonrestrictive) relative clauses—clauses that merely add extra information:

NONESSENTIAL CLAUSE

First prize went to the longhaired collie, *which came all the way from Hartford.*
[It was the only longhaired collie in the competition.]

ESSENTIAL CLAUSE

First prize went to the longhaired collie *which came all the way from Hartford.*
[There were other longhaired collies in the competition.]

 10e Use the subjective case when a pronoun functions as a sentence subject, clause subject, or subject complement

Case refers to the form a pronoun takes to indicate its grammatical relation to other words in a sentence.

The **subjective case** (*I, you, he, she, it, we they, who, whoever*) is required for all pronouns used as subjects, including pronouns that are paired with a noun to form a compound subject or to rename the noun (see 10g).

She and Octavio are good friends.   [Sentence subject]

It seems that only Harrison and *I* were not invited.   [Clause subject]

In predicate nominative constructions, the verb *be* is used to set up an "equation" between a noun subject or a pronoun subject such as *it, that, this* and a personal pronoun such as *he, she, it,* or *they*.

>   *she*
> "Hello, is Carol there?" "Yes, this is ~~her~~."

>   *he* *I*
> Who will be the lead actor—~~him~~ or ~~me~~?

10f Use the objective case when a pronoun functions as an object .

The **objective case** (*me, you, him, her, it, us, them, whom, whomever*) is required for all pronouns used as objects, indirect objects, and objects of prepositions, including any pronoun paired with a noun or another pronoun to form a compound object.

> The boss invited Janice and *him* to lunch.   [Pronoun as indirect object]

> Just between *you* and *me*, don't you think Marty's been a little out of line lately?   [Pronoun as object of a preposition]

10g Test for pronoun case in compound constructions by using the pronoun alone

Most problems with pronoun case arise in compound constructions, when a pronoun is paired with a noun:

> The instructor gave Natasha and [*me, I*] an extra project to do.

In such sentences, the case of the pronoun—subjective or objective—depends on its function in the sentence. If you are unsure about which case to use, the best way to find out is to try the sentence without the noun:

> The instructor gave [*me, I*] an extra project to do.

Seeing it in this form makes it easier to decide what the correct form is:

> The instructor gave Natasha and *me* an extra project to do.

A special type of pronoun-noun pairing, called an **appositive,** occurs when a pronoun is conjoined with a noun.

We Americans tend to be patriotic.

Sometimes people from other countries complain about *us Americans.*

Again, if you are unsure about which case to use in such situations, just omit the noun and see which pronoun form is correct.

We tend to be patriotic.

Sometimes people from other countries complain about *us.*

10h Choose the form for an interrogative or relative pronoun based on how it functions in its clause

The pronouns *who, whom, whoever, whomever,* and *whose* are used in questions and relative clauses (see 9c-3). In questions, they are called **interrogative pronouns**; in clauses, they are called **relative pronouns.**

Who reserved this book?   [Interrogative pronoun]

I'd like to find the person *who* reserved this book.   [Relative pronoun]

When you ask a question and reverse normal sentence word order, choosing the correct interrogative pronoun can be puzzling. As a writer, you must decide whether the *wh-* pronoun functions as a subject or an object in the clause in which it is used.

[*Who, Whom*] are you going to invite to the wedding?

10i Use possessive pronouns to show ownership

There are two types of possessive pronouns. **Attributive possessive pronouns** (*my, your, her, his, its, our, their*) are used directly before a noun, while nominal possessive pronouns (*mine, yours, hers, his, its, ours, theirs*) are used with a linking verb (*is, was*).

This is *my* car.

This car is *mine.*

10j Choose the case for a pronoun in a comparison based on how it would function in its own clause

What is the meaning of this sentence?

Mark likes school more than me.

Technically, it means that Mark has a greater liking for school than he does for the speaker of the sentence. It does not mean that Mark has a greater liking for school than the speaker does. The latter meaning is correctly expressed with this construction:

Mark likes school more than I.

You can avoid this problem by recognizing that the second part of the comparison (the part after *than*) is an incomplete clause. The complete versions of the two sentences make the distinction clear:

Mark likes school more than [he likes] me.

Mark likes school more than I [like school].

A similar procedure can be used with *as . . . as* constructions.

VERBS

Using verbs correctly can help make writing lively and precise. This section explains some of the major aspects of verb usage: form, tense, voice, and mood. (Two other aspects, gender and number, are discussed in 10a.)

10k Learn the regular verb forms

All verbs in English, except *be*, have five basic forms or **principal parts.**

Base form	Present tense (-s form)	Past tense	Past participle	Present participle
jump	jumps	jumped	jumped	jumping
erase	erases	erased	erased	erasing
veto	vetoes	vetoed	vetoed	vetoing

Most English verbs are **regular verbs.** Their forms follow the pattern of the preceding examples: adding *s* (or *es*) to the base form to make the third-person singular present tense, adding *d* (or *ed*) to make the past tense and past participle, and adding *ing* to the base form (and sometimes dropping the final *e*) to make the present participle.

The base form, or simple form, of a verb is the form listed in a dictionary, the form normally used with plural nouns or the pronouns *I, you, we,* or *they* in the present tense: "Hummingbirds *migrate* south in winter." "I *walk* two miles every day."

When the subject of a sentence is *he, she, it,* or some other third-person singular subject, the **present tense** of the verb has an *s* added to it: "She *visits* New York every month." "My neighbor *walks* laps around our block." Sometimes a slight change is required in the spelling of the base form (*fly/flies, veto/vetoes*).

The **past tense** of a verb is used to describe action that occurred in the past. For a regular verb, add *d* or *ed* to the base form to get the past tense: "Fox TV *televised* Super Bowl XXXI." "We *wanted* to see the game."

The **past participle** of a regular verb is similar in form to the past tense. The past participle can be used (1) with *has* or *have* in the present perfect tense, (2) with *had* in the past perfect tense, (3) with some form of *be* to create a passive-voice construction, and (4) by itself, as an adjective, to modify a noun.

We *have petitioned* the school board for a new crosswalk.   [Present perfect]

Before last night's meeting, we *had talked* about going directly to the mayor.   [Past perfect]

Last year, two students *were injured* trying to cross this street.   [Passive voice]

The parents of the *injured* students are supporting our cause.   [Adjective]

The **present participle** is created by adding *ing* to the base form of a verb. It is used (1) with some form of *be* to indicate ongoing action (the progressive tense), (2) as a gerund, and (3) as an adjective.

Joaquin *is working* on a new project.   [Progressive tense]

He enjoys *working*.   [Gerund]

This is a *working* draft of my paper.   [Adjective]

10l Learn common irregular verb forms

An **irregular verb** is one whose past tense and past participle do not follow the standard pattern of being created by adding *d* or *ed* to the base form. A few common irregular verbs and their past tense and past participle forms include:

Base form	Past tense	Past participle
be	was, were	been
go	went	gone
swim	swam	swum

10m Know how to use auxiliary verbs

An **auxiliary verb** (or **helping verb**) is one that is used with a main verb to indicate tense, mood, or voice. The most common auxiliary verbs are *be*, *have*, and *do*.

> She *is finishing* her paper. [Progressive tense, indicating ongoing action]
>
> The college *has adopted* a new honor code. [Present perfect tense, indicating past action with ongoing effects]
>
> We *do need* to get going. [Emphasis]
>
> My roommate *has been asked* to run for the student senate. [Passive voice, present perfect tense]
>
> *Does* he *know* what's involved? [Question]

Other important helping verbs are the **modal auxiliary verbs** (*may/might, can/could, will/would, shall/should, must, ought to,* and *have to*). These verbs communicate degrees of probability, necessity, or obligation. A modal auxiliary verb is used only with the base form of another verb:

> The concert *might be* sold out.
>
> We *should get* tickets before it is too late.

Modal auxiliaries can be used with forms of *be*, *have*, or *do*, but not with other modal auxiliaries.

NONSTANDARD   We might *could* do that.

REVISED   We might *be able to* do that.   [Verb phrase substituted]

In some cases, you can simply eliminate one of the modal auxiliaries:

NONSTANDARD   Sally *should ought to* cancel her appointment.

REVISED   Sally *should* cancel her appointment.

OR

Sally *ought* to cancel her appointment.

10n Learn the verb tenses

Verb tense expresses the time of the action or the state of being indicated by a verb. English has three basic tenses: past, present, and future. Each tense can also take on a **verbal aspect**, indicating duration or completion of the verb's action or state of being. The three verbal aspects in English are progressive, perfect, and perfect progressive. With all possible combinations of tenses and aspects, English has twelve verb tenses.

1 Present tenses

The simple present tense is used to express a general truth, to make an observation, or to describe an habitual activity: "A rolling stone *gathers* no moss." "Oates's stories *depress* me." With an appropriate time expression, the simple present can be used to refer to a scheduled future event: "The show *begins* in five minutes." The simple present is used in stage directions and in critical discussions of literary works: "In *The Tempest*, all the action *occurs* in one place during one day." The simple present also is used to express a scientific fact or law: "Water *boils* at 100° Celsius."

The **present progressive tense** is formed with the auxiliary verb *am, are,* or *is* and the present participle (*-ing* form) of a main verb. The present progressive is used to indicate action occurring at the present time: "Jennifer *is preparing* for the MCAT exam." With an appropriate time expression, the present progressive can be used to announce future events: "A new supermarket *is opening* next week."

The **present perfect tense** is formed with the auxiliary verb *have* or *has* and the past participle of a main verb. The present perfect is used to indicate action that began in the past and either is continuing or has continuing effects in the present: "Many people *have expressed* alarm about environmental degradation."

The **present perfect progressive tense** is formed by combining *have been* or *has been* with the present participle of a main verb. The present perfect progressive is used similarly to the present perfect but emphasizes the ongoing nature of the activity: Eric *has been studying* German for two years.

2 Past tenses

The simple past tense is used to describe actions or conditions that occurred or applied entirely in the past: "In 1950, the United States *consisted* of only forty-eight states."

The **past progressive tense** is formed by combining the auxiliary verb *was* or *were* with the present participle of a main verb. The past progressive describes action continuing over a period of time in the past. It is often used to set the stage for another action of shorter duration: "He *was cleaning* the living room when the phone rang."

The **past perfect tense** is created by combining the auxiliary verb *had* with the past participle of a main verb. The past perfect is used to describe a past action that preceded another past action: "Before her accident, Amanda *had thought* of taking the job."

The **past perfect progressive tense** functions like the past perfect tense but puts more emphasis on the continuing or repetitive nature of the past action. The past perfect progressive is formed by combining *had been* with the present participle of a main verb: "Before her accident, Amanda *had been thinking* of taking the job."

3 Future tenses

The simple future tense, as its name implies, expresses actions or conditions that will occur in the future. The simple future consists of the modal auxiliary verb *will* and the base form of a main verb: "Ames *will be* a half hour late."

The **future progressive tense** is formed by combining *will be* with the present participle of a main verb. The future progressive expresses action that will be continuing or repeated in the future: "Next year my son *will be going* to college."

The **future perfect tense** consists of *will have* and the past participle of a main verb. The future perfect is used to describe an action that will occur in the future but before some specified time: "By the end of this year, gun-related violence *will have doubled.*"

The **future perfect progressive tense** is similar to the future perfect but emphasizes the continuous or repetitive nature of the action. The future perfect progressive consists of *will have been* plus the present participle of a main verb: "By next year, I *will have been working* for fifteen years."

10o   Observe sequence of tenses

Good writing presents a coherent framework of time. Since time is indicated in part by verb tense, it is important to select verb tenses carefully and logically. The relationship between two or more verbs in the same sentence or in adjacent sentences is called the **sequence of tenses.**

1 Sequence of verb tenses in compound or adjacent sentences

Two or more independent clauses about closely related events or situations may be connected by a coordinating conjunction (*and, or, but*) to form a compound sentence. Alternatively, two related independent clauses may be presented as consecutive sentences. Typically, the main verbs in each clause or sentence have the same tense: "Joe *wants* to go to the game, but Lori *does* not."

2 Sequence of verb tenses in complex sentences

A complex sentence has one independent clause and one or more dependent clauses. Each clause has its own main verb. The appropriate tense for each main verb depends on the context and the intended meaning. If the actions expressed by these verbs occur at approximately the same time, the verbs should be in the same tense: "Before you *sit* down, *adjust* the height of your chair."

When you need to make it clear that one past action or event preceded another, use the past perfect or past perfect progressive tense in one clause and the simple past tense in the other clause: "Amanda *had thought* of taking the job, but now she *said* no." When you need to show that a past action or event preceded a present or future one, use the present perfect or present perfect progressive tense to express the past action or event: "Since the Pope *has been* to Mexico already, he probably *will* not *go* again."

3 Sequence of verb tenses with infinitives

There are two kinds of **infinitives:** the **present infinitive** (the base form of a verb, often preceded by *to*) and the **perfect infinitive** (*to have* plus the past participle of a verb) (see 9a-4). Use the present infinitive for an action that occurs at the same time as or later than the action expressed by the main verb: "Samantha *wants* me *to pick up* the car." Use the perfect infinitive for an action that occurs prior to the action expressed by the main verb: "Samantha *wants* me *to have picked up* the car."

4 Sequence of verb tenses with participles

The **present participle** (the *-ing* form of a verb) can be used to represent an action that occurs at the same time as that expressed by the main verb: "*Walking* into the house, Jim sensed danger."

The **past participle** is used to indicate that an action occurs before or during the action expressed by the main verb: "*Stung* by criticism of his latest film, Costner is working hard on a new one."

The **present perfect participle** (*having* plus the past participle) expresses an action occurring prior to the action of the main verb: "*Having signed* a contract, Deanna was left with no options."

10p Use transitive and intransitive verbs correctly: *sit/set, lie/lay, rise/raise*

A **transitive verb** is a verb that takes a direct object (see 9a-3). In other words, a transitive verb transfers an action from a subject to an object. The sentence "A virus damaged my hard drive" has a transitive verb (*damaged*) that transfers the action to the direct object (*hard drive*). Some typical transitive verbs are *see, hear, consult, kick, recognize,* and *mix.* Transitive verbs are usually marked in dictionaries with the abbreviation *vt* or *tr.*

An **intransitive verb** is one that does not take a direct object. Some typical intransitive verbs are *sleep, relax, die, go, fall, come,* and *walk.* Intransitive verbs are usually identified in dictionaries by the abbreviation *vi* or *intr.*

Many speakers of English confuse *sit* and *set*, *lie* and *lay*, and *rise* and *raise*. The two verbs in each of these pairs sound somewhat alike and have related meanings, but they differ as to whether they can take an object. The first member of each pair is intransitive and cannot take an object; the second member is transitive and does take an object.

INTRANSITIVE   Jorge *will sit* over there.   [The verb has no object.]

TRANSITIVE   Jorge *will set* the *flowers* over there.   [The verb has an object, *flowers*.]

10q Favor active over passive voice

Voice is the characteristic of a verb that indicates whether the subject of a sentence is acting or being acted upon. In the **active voice**, the subject of the sentence performs an action on a direct object (see 9b). In the **passive voice**, the subject of the sentence is acted upon. Only transitive verbs can be cast in active and passive voice (see 10p).

ACTIVE   Subject/actor   DO
My friend Julie *handcrafted* this pin.   [The subject acts on an object.]

PASSIVE   Subject   DO/actor
This pin *was handcrafted* by my friend Julie.   [The subject is acted upon by the object following the verb.]

The passive voice consists of an appropriate form of the auxiliary verb *be* and the past participle of a main verb (see 10k). A passive-voice sentence may refer to the performer of the action in a *by* phrase following the verb. In practice, though, the *by* phrase is often omitted, which has the effect of concealing or deemphasizing the performer of the action: "This pin *was handcrafted*."

In general, good writers favor the active voice over the passive voice. The active voice is more concise and more direct—and

WEBLINK

http://ccc.commnet.edu/
grammar/verbs.htm#verb

A superb resource on verbs, including quizzes and lots of cool graphics thus more vigorous—than the passive. In some cases, however, the passive voice works better than the active voice.

10r Make sure verbs are in the proper mood

The **mood** of a verb indicates the type of statement being made by the sentence—an assertion, a question, a command, a wish, or a hypothetical condition. English verbs have three moods: indicative, imperative, and subjunctive.

The **indicative mood** is used to make assertions, state opinions, and ask questions. It is the most commonly used mood in English.

Washington *was* the first president of the United States.   [Assertion]

Citizens *should take* more interest in local government.   [Opinion]

Do you *want* to vote? [Question]

The **imperative mood** is used to express commands and give instructions. Commands are always addressed to a second person, although the explicit *you* is normally omitted. Instructions are often cast in the imperative mood. "*Insert* Setup Disk 1 in the drive. Then *run* the program."

The **subjunctive mood** is used for hypothetical conditions, polite requests, wishes, and other uncertain statements. A verb in the subjunctive mood often appears in dependent clauses beginning with *if* or *that*. The present subjunctive is the same as the base form of the verb. The past subjunctive is identical to the past tense of the verb. The only exception is *were*, which is used for all subjunctive uses of *be* except after verbs of requesting, requiring, or recommending, where *be* is used: "I wish I *were* an A student!" "She asked that her client *be* given probation." The past perfect subjunctive has the same form as the ordinary past perfect.

1 Hypothetical *if* constructions

When an *if* clause expresses a contrary-to-fact or unreal condition, the verb of the clause should be in the past subjunctive or past perfect subjunctive mood. The main clause verb should include that modal auxiliary *would, could,* or *might*.

If I *were* you, I *would* make up my Incompletes as soon as possible.
[Expresses a hypothetical future condition]

If John *had been* there, he *might* have been able to help.   [Expresses a
hypothetical past condition]

Do not use *would, could,* or *might* in a hypothetical *if* clause. In contrary-
to-fact sentences, modal auxiliaries such as *would* and *could* belong in the main
clause, not in the conditional (subordinate) clause. Use the subjunctive in the
conditional clause.

SUBJUNCTIVE FORM REVISED

          lived
If we ~~would live~~ closer to San Francisco, we would go there more often.

2 Dependent clauses expressing a wish

In a dependent clause following the verb *wish*, use the past subjunctive for
present contrary-to-fact conditions and the past perfect subjunctive for past
contrary-to-fact conditions: "I wish [that] he *were* here." "I wish [that] he *had
stayed*."

3 Dependent clauses expressing a request, suggestion,
  or demand

Verbs like *require, demand, suggest,* and *insist* are usually followed by a dependent clause beginning with *that*. The verb in the *that* clause should be in
the subjunctive mood: "The police require that all pets *be* kept on a leash."
Sometimes *that* is omitted.

ADJECTIVES AND ADVERBS

Using adjective and adverbs allows writers to add details to their work, making it more precise and colorful. But adjectives and adverbs have their proper
uses, and it is important not to confuse them or use them incorrectly.

10s Use adjectives to modify nouns

An **adjective** is a word that modifies a noun (see 9a-5). Typically, adjectives answer one of the following questions: which? what kind? how many? Sometimes an adjective is placed next to the noun it modifies, either directly before the noun (an *ancient* building, the *first* page) or directly after (a dream *forsaken*, his curiosity *satisfied*). Other times an adjective is separated from the noun it modifies, as in the sentence "The movie was *exciting*." In these cases, a linking verb (such as *is, was,* or *seemed*) connects the noun and its modifier to form a predicate adjective and a subject complement.

WEBLINK

http://www.uottawa.ca/
academic/arts/writcent/
hypergrammar/adjective
.html

A complete discussion of
adjectives

10t Avoid overuse of nouns as modifiers

A noun can modify another noun to form a noun compound that functions as an adjective. Some examples are *park* bench, *soda* pop, *letter* opener, *telephone* book, *fender* bender, *tape* player, and *movie* theater.

Noun compounding can help you save a few words—*windshield* is more concise than *shield against the wind*—but it can be confusing for readers, especially if you use more than three nouns in a row. To avoid long noun strings like *the picnic table cross brace,* use a prepositional phrase: *the cross brace under the picnic table.* Such phrasing may take a few more words, but the meaning will be clearer.

10u Use adverbs to modify verbs, adjectives, other adverbs, and clauses

An adverb is a word that modifies a verb, an adjective, another adverb, or a clause (see 9a-6). Adverbs modify verbs by answering such questions as these: when? how? how often? where? to what degree?

Linda *often* goes to the gym to work out.   [Modifies the verb *goes*]

They made a *very* bad mistake.   [Modifies the adjective *bad*]

The car was turned *almost* upside down.   [Modifies the adverb *upside down*]

Luckily, I was able to find a backup disk.   [Modifies the entire clause]

10v   Be aware of some commonly confused adjectives and adverbs

The pairs of words *good/well* and *bad/badly* are misused by many writers who fail to recognize that *good* and *bad* are adjectives, whereas *well* and *badly* are adverbs. The sentence "Fielder runs *good* for a man his size" is ungrammatical. The correct version is

Fielder runs *well* for a man his size.   [The adverb *well* modifies the verb *runs*.]

The adjective *good* is appropriate when the word being modified is a noun.

He has a *good*, long stride.   [The adjective *good* modifies the noun *stride*.]

When the main verb expresses a feeling or a perception (such verbs include *look, appear, feel, seem, taste,* and *smell*), the correct modifier is an adjective complement.

I feel *bad* about what I did.   [Not *badly*; the adjective *bad* modifies the noun *I*.]

This gazpacho tastes *good*.   [Not *well*; the adjective *good* modifies the noun *gazpacho*.]

10w   Use comparative and superlative forms of adjectives and adverbs correctly

Most adjectives and a few adverbs can be used to make comparisons.

Ted works *hard*. He is *determined* to get ahead.   [Positive form]

Ted works *harder* than I do. He is *more determined* than I am. [Comparative forms]

Ted works the *hardest* of anybody I know. He is the *most determined* person I have ever met. [Superlative forms]

When making comparisons, be accurate, complete, and logical. When comparing two items, use the comparative form. When comparing three or more items, use the superlative form.

Of the two candidates, I like Johnson *better*.

Of the three candidates, I like Johnson *best*.

Use *few, fewer,* or *fewest* with count nouns (such as *books, calories, flowers,* and *dollars*). Use *little, less,* or *least* with noncount nouns (such as *water, understanding,* and *progress*).

The team has *fewer* fans than it used to have.

The new package contains *less* rice.

Make sure the terms of a comparison are complete. Do not write a sentence like "This headache remedy works better." Many readers will wonder, "Better than what?" Including a *than* phrase as part of the comparison makes it clear:

This headache remedy works better *than any other*.

10x Avoid double negatives

A **double negative** is a sentence or phrase containing two negative modifiers (typically adverbs such as *never, no, not, hardly, barely,* and *scarcely*) that carry the same meaning. Double negatives are considered nonstandard in modern English and should be avoided in formal writing and speaking.

The city buses do not have ~~no~~ *any* lifts for disabled passengers.

The passengers ~~can't~~ *can* hardly get on board.

CHAPTER **11**

Sentence Fragments, Comma Splices, and Run-On Sentences

Now that you have learned grammar rules about individual parts of speech, you have mastered common sentence structure. This chapter covers the problems of sentence fragments, comma splices, and run-on sentences.

SENTENCE FRAGMENTS

A fragment is a grammatically incomplete sentence. Complete sentences (1) have a complete predicate, (2) have a grammatical subject, and (3) do not begin with a subordinating conjunction or relative pronoun unless they are connected to a main clause.

11a Make sentences grammatically complete

If you have a good style/grammar checker in your computer, it should identify most of the sentence fragments in your writing. But it will not be able to tell you how to fix them. So, you will need to solve these problems on your own.

1 Does the sentence have a complete predicate?

In standard English, all sentences must have a complete predicate—that is, a main verb plus any necessary helping verbs and complements. The main verb must be a *finite* verb, not an infinitive (*to* form) or a gerund (*-ing* form).

The second part of the following example has been incorrectly set off as a separate sentence; it does not have a finite verb and so cannot be a full sentence:

Seven is a very symbolic number in Judeo-Christian culture.
Appearing often in the Bible and other sacred texts.

Simply replacing the period with a comma will correct the problem:

Seven is a very symbolic number in Judeo-Christian culture, appearing
often in the Bible and other sacred texts.

2 Does the sentence have a subject?

In standard English, all sentences (except commands) must have a grammatical subject.

Sometimes, a fragment can be corrected by simply inserting an appropriate subject and making other related changes:

Most of today's sitcoms are not about families in suburbia.
Rather, they are
~~But rather~~ about young adults in the big city.

Sometimes, simply changing the punctuation and making the fragment part of the previous sentence will correct the error:

, but
Most of today's sitcoms are not about families in suburbia. ~~But~~ rather about
young adults in the big city.

By removing the period after *suburbia*, you enable *most of today's sitcoms* to serve as the subject for the rest of the sentence, thereby eliminating the fragment.

3 Are the subordinating phrases or clauses connected to a main clause?

Check to be sure that word clusters beginning with a subordinating conjunction (such as *because, although,* or *if*) or a relative pronoun (such as *which, who,* or *that*) are connected or subordinated to a main subject and predicate.

11b Connect dependent clauses

Dependent clauses have a subject and a predicate but are linked to a main clause with a subordinating conjunction (such as *because, although,* or *if*) or a relative pronoun (such as *which, who,* or *that*). Because dependent clauses depend for their meaning on their connection to a main clause, they cannot stand alone. Therefore, if you begin a clause with a subordinating conjunction or relative pronoun and then end it with a period or semicolon before connecting it to a main clause, you have produced a fragment, not a sentence. In the following sentence, changing the period to a comma allows the *Before* clause to serve as a dependent clause linked to *I must first discuss . . .,* the main clause.

> *Before I delve into critically analyzing the characters,/ I must first discuss the opening sequence.*

Likewise, relative clauses also need to be connected to a main clause. In the following sentence, the solution is simply to eliminate the period, joining the two clauses:

> *may*
> What seems annoying to me. ~~May~~ not bother you at all.

11c   Connect phrases

Phrases are similar to clauses except that they lack full verbs. Phrases can be used as modifiers, subjects, objects, or complements—but never as sentences. Make sure that all of your phrases are connected to main clauses.

> Many nations began to process their own food, minerals, and other
> *, using*
> raw materials. ~~Using~~ *foreign aid and investments to back their efforts.*

COMMA SPLICES AND RUN-ON SENTENCES

Joining two independent clauses with a comma creates a **comma splice.** Putting two independent clauses together without a conjunction or any punctuation creates a **run-on sentence** (or fused sentence).

Run-on sentences are incorrect in standard English and are often confusing to readers. There are four main ways to correct comma splices and run-on sentences:

WEBLINK

http://ccc.commnet.edu/grammar/runons.htm

All you need to know about comma splices and run-on sentences, with exercises

- Turn one clause into a subordinate clause.
- Add a comma and a coordinating conjunction.
- Separate the clauses with a semicolon.
- Separate the clauses with a period.

11d Turn one clause into a subordinate clause

Often the best way to correct a comma splice or run-on sentence is to convert one of the two clauses into a subordinate clause. This can be done by using either a subordinating conjunction (such as *while, although, because,* or *if*) or a relative pronoun (such as *which, that,* or *who*).

> The best keyboard for one-handed users is the Dvorak keyboard, ~~it~~ *which* has a more convenient layout than the standard Qwerty keyboard.

Sometimes this technique may require switching the two clauses around:

> *Because* it has a more convenient layout than the standard Qwerty keyboard, the best keyboard for one-handed users is the Dvorak keyboard.

11e Separate clauses with a comma and a coordinating conjunction

If the two parts of a comma splice or run-on sentence are of equal importance, you can put a comma and a coordinating conjunction (such as *and, or, but, nor,* or *yet*) between them:

^; but

An eagle once flew past our house ^I only got a brief glimpse

of it.

Simply inserting a comma in a run-on sentence is not enough, for that only produces another error (a comma splice); you must also insert a conjunction.

11f Separate independent clauses with a semicolon

If the two parts of a comma splice or run-on sentence are of equal importance, you can insert a semicolon between them.

;

Desktop computers usually have bigger screens than laptops do ^/ laptops are easier to carry around.

If you use a conjunctive adverb such as *however, therefore,* or *for example,* be sure to place the semicolon before it:

;

Laptops are coming down in price ^/ *therefore,* more people are

buying them.

11g Separate independent clauses with a period

Often the easiest way to correct a comma splice or run-on sentence is by inserting a period between the two independent clauses:

Dvorak keyboards put the most frequently typed characters within

. They

easy reach ^~~they~~ are often used in speed-typing competitions.

CHAPTER **12**

Subject-Verb Agreement

Subjects and verbs should agree in number; that is, they must both be either singular or plural. "He go to work at nine o'clock" is ungrammatical because *he* is singular and *go* (in the third person) is plural. Here are some rules on subject-verb **agreement.**

12a Use plural verbs with plural subjects; singular verbs with singular subjects

He <u>goes</u> to work at nine o'clock.

We <u>see</u> each other later in the day.

With a modified subject, be sure the verb agrees with the simple subject.

Meg's <u>circle</u> of friends <u>gives</u> her a lot of support. [*Circle* is the simple subject of the phrase *Meg's circle of friends.*]

12b Use plural verbs with most compound subjects

Compound subjects refer to two or more people, places, or things and are formed with the conjunction *and*. In most cases, compound subjects have a plural sense and thus require plural verbs.

<u>Geography and history</u> <u>are</u> my favorite subjects.

> **WEBLINK**
>
> http://ccc.commnet.edu/
> grammar/sv_agr.htm
>
> A great guide to subject/
> verb agreement, complete
> with quizzes and exercises

12c Make the verb agree with the closest part of a disjunctive subject

A **disjunctive subject** consists of two nouns or pronouns jointed by *or* or *nor*. The verb in a sentence with such a subject agrees with the second part of the subject.

> Either my sister or my <u>parents <u>are</u></u> coming.

> Neither my parents nor my <u>sister <u>is</u></u> coming.

If the singular verb sounds awkward to you with such a mixed subject, you can switch the two parts of the subject and use the plural form of the verb:

> Neither my sister nor my <u>parents <u>are</u></u> coming.

12d Make the verb agree in number with the sense of the indefinite pronoun

Indefinite pronouns include *anybody, everyone, nothing, each,* and *much.* Unlike regular pronouns, they do not necessarily refer to any particular person or thing. Most indefinite pronouns are grammatically singular. Therefore, when used as subjects, they should have singular verbs.

> <u>No one <u>is</u></u> here.

> <u>Something</u> <u>needs</u> to be done about this.

> <u>Each</u> of the candidates <u>is</u> giving a short speech.

A few indefinite pronouns, including *both* and *others,* are plural and therefore require plural verbs. Other indefinite pronouns, such as *some, all, any, more,* and *none,* can be used with either singular or plural verb forms, depending on what they refer to.

> <u>All</u> of the members <u>were</u> at the meeting. [*All* refers to plural *members.*]

> <u>All</u> of their attention <u>was</u> directed at her. [*All* refers to singular *attention.*]

12e Use singular verbs with most collective nouns

Collective nouns are words such as *team, faculty, jury,* and *committee,* which can have either a singular or a plural sense depending on whether they refer to the group or to the individuals within the group (see 9a-1). These nouns usually take singular verbs.

The team is doing better than expected.

The band seems to be road-weary.

To emphasize the plural sense of collective nouns, simply insert an appropriate plural noun.

The band members seem to be road-weary.

12f Use singular verbs with nouns that are plural in form but singular in sense

Words such as *mathematics, athletics, politics, economics, physics,* and *news* look like plural nouns because of the *-s* ending. However, these nouns are usually singular in meaning and thus require singular verbs.

Economics is my favorite subject.

The news from Lake Wobegon always interests me.

12g Be sure a linking verb agrees with its subject

Sometimes you may find yourself faced with a sentence of the form "X is Y," in which the subject X is singular and the subject complement Y is plural, or vice versa. In such cases, the linking verb should agree in number with the subject, not with the subject complement (see 9b-3).

Her main interest is boys.

Boys are her main interest.

> **12h** **Make the verb agree with its true subject, not the expletive *here* or *there***

In a sentence beginning with *here* or *there* and some form of the verb *be*, the true (grammatical) subject is usually the noun that immediately follows the *be* verb form.

There are some people at the door.

Here is the address you were looking for.

CHAPTER 13

Misplaced and Dangling Modifiers

Modifiers are words, phrases, or clauses that qualify other words, phrases, or clauses. Used properly, modifiers can make writing richer and more precise.

> **13a** Position modifiers close to the words they modify

For maximum clarity, modifiers should be placed as close as possible to (ideally, right next to) the words they modify.

Unlike George,
    Kramer does not need the approval of anyone, ~~unlike George.~~

     frequently
Businesses publish the URLs for their Web sites ~~frequently~~ in advertisements.

13b Avoid ambiguity

A modifier that is not carefully positioned may present the reader with two or more possible interpretations.

> Bound, gagged, and trussed up nude in a denim bag with plugs in her ears and tape over her eyes, Cleveland teacher Brenda P. Noonan told yesterday how she was kidnapped and taken to Florida without knowing where she was going or why.
>
> —Quoted in Richard Lederer,
> *Anguished English*

WEBLINK

http://www.uottawa.ca/
academic/arts/writcent/
hypergrammar/msplmod
.html

How not to use misplaced
and dangling modifiers in
your writing

It must have been quite a trick to describe these things while being bound and gagged! The following version of the sentence is clearer:

> Cleveland teacher Brenda P. Noonan told yesterday how she was kidnapped and taken to Florida bound, gagged, and trussed up nude in a denim bag with plugs in her ears and tape over her eyes, without knowing where she was going or why.

13c Try to put lengthy modifiers at the beginning or end

When a lengthy modifier is placed in the middle of a sentence, it tends to disrupt the basic structure (subject-verb-complement) of the sentence. By moving such modifiers to the beginning or end of the sentence, you preserve the basic structure and make the sentence more readable.

MODIFIER IN THE MIDDLE OF THE SENTENCE

> A television network usually, *after it airs a documentary*, makes the film available to groups for a nominal rental fee.

REVISED

> *After it airs a documentary,* a television network usually makes the film available to groups for a nominal rental fee.

13d Avoid disruptive modifiers

English sentences are made up of subgroupings of words, such as the verb and its object or the word *to* and the rest of the infinitive construction. When modifiers are inserted into these subgroupings, there is a risk of interrupting and obscuring the vital connections between key words.

1 Modifiers between the verb and its object

Readers like to be able to move easily through the main predicate of a sentence, going from verb to object without interruption. For this reason, it is best to avoid inserting any interupting modifiers between the verb and its object.

> The magician␣ shuffled *quickly* the cards.
> ∧*quickly*

2 Split infinitives

Some readers prefer to see both parts of an infinitive construction (*to escape*) together, as in "He hoped *to escape* easily." Other readers will accept a one-word interruption between parts, or split infinitive, as in "He hoped *to* easily *escape*." Almost all readers have difficulty comprehending an infinitive construction when its parts are split with a longer phrase, as in "He hoped *to* easily and quickly *escape*."

SPLIT INFINITIVES REVISED

> Star Trekkers hope to␣ *boldly, loyally, and optimistically* go where none have
> ∧*go*
> gone before.   [With all due respect for the original motto, too many modifiers splitting the infinitive here interrupt the sense of the sentence.]

13e Avoid dangling modifiers

A mistake that plagues many writers is the use of the **dangling modifier,** an introductory verbal phrase that does not have a clear referent.

> *Breaking in through the window of the girls' dormitory*, the dean of men surprised ten members of the football team.
>
> —Quoted in Richard Lederer, *Anguished English*

Did the dean break into the girls' dormitory? To prevent this misinterpretation, the writer should have put the real culprits in the subject position of the main clause.

> Breaking in through the window of the girls' dormitory, ten members of the football team were surprised by the dean of men.

It will not do simply to mention the missing agent somewhere in the main clause; the referent must be in the subject position.

CHAPTER 14

Faulty Shifts

Readers expect writers to use a consistent focus, time frame, and tone. Writers should try to satisfy this expectation by avoiding unnecessary shifts.

14a Avoid shifts in focus

The *focus* of a piece of writing is what or whom the writing is about. It is indicated usually by the choice of point of view, as expressed by a singular or plural subject pronoun: first person (*I, we*), second person (*you*), or third person (*he, she, it, they*). A first-person focus is an appropriate point of view for personal narratives and informal correspondence; a second-person focus is appropriate for instructions; a third-person focus is appropriate for most academic, professional, and other types of formal writing. Shifting from one focus to another can be confusing to readers.

> You should start writing a paper well before the deadline; otherwise, ~~one~~ *you* may end up doing it at the last minute, with no chance to revise it.

14b   Avoid unnecessary shifts in verb tense and mood

Verb tense indicates the time frame of an action (see 10n). Unless you are describing a situation where there is a natural or logical difference in time frames, it is best to use the same verb tense throughout.

WEBLINK

http://owl.english.purdue
.edu/handouts/esl/
esltensverb.html

How to avoid inappropriate shifts of verb tense

In 1995, the median pay for full-time female workers in the United States was $22,497, while the median pay for males was $31,496. In other words, women ~~make~~ *made* 71 cents to a man's dollar.

There are three **moods** in English: indicative, imperative, and subjunctive. The **indicative mood** is used for facts and assertions, the **imperative mood** for commands, and the **subjunctive mood** for conditions that are contrary to fact (see 10r). If you mix moods in the same sentence, you may confuse your readers:

INCONSISTENT MOOD

> If China were a democracy, it will have elections at periodic intervals.

REVISED

> If China *is* a democracy, *it will have* elections at periodic intervals.   [Both verbs are in the indicative, suggesting a factual assertion.]

If China *were* a democracy, it *would have* elections at periodic intervals.   [Both verbs are in the subjunctive, indicating a contrary-to-fact condition.]

14c Avoid shifts in tone

Tone refers to the writer's attitude toward the subject matter or the audience. It can be formal or informal, ironic or direct, friendly or hostile, and so on. Since readers need to get a clear sense of what the writer's attitude is, a writer should strive to maintain a consistent authorial tone.

INCONSISTENT TONE

The world of folklore and fairy tales is one that attracts adults and children alike. As adults, we look back fondly on childhood cartoons and still get a kick out of 'em.

REVISED FROM COLLOQUIAL TO FORMAL

The world of folklore and fairy tales is one that attracts adults and children alike. As adults, we look back fondly on childhood cartoons and find them as enjoyable as ever.

14d Avoid mixed constructions

Mixed constructions result when a writer starts a sentence in a certain way but then changes track and finishes it differently. The two parts of the sentence end up being incompatible—and confusing to the reader.

MIXED   In the world created by movies and television makes fiction seem like reality.

REVISED   The world created by movies and television makes fiction seem like reality.

OR   In the world created by movies and television, fiction seems like reality.

14e Create consistency between subjects and predicates

Subjects and predicates should always harmonize, both logically and grammatically. When they do not, the result is faulty predication.

FAULTY   Writer's block is when you cannot get started writing.

In this sentence, a noun (*writer's block*) is compared to an adverb of time (*when . . .*).

REVISED $\overset{N}{Writer's\ block\ is\ a\ condition}$ in which you cannot get started writing.

14f Avoid unmarked shifts between direct and indirect discourse

Direct discourse is language that is taken word for word from another source and thus is enclosed in quotation marks. **Indirect discourse** is language that is paraphrased and therefore is *not* enclosed in quotation marks. If you shift from one mode to the other, you may have to alter not only punctuation but also pronouns and verb tenses so as not to confuse your readers.

CONFUSING   Agassiz, the legendary Swiss scientist and teacher, once said I cannot afford to waste my time making money.   [Without quotation marks, this statement seems to refer to two different people: Agassiz and the writer.]

REVISED   Agassiz, the legendary Swiss scientist and teacher, once said that *he could not* afford to waste his time making money.   [By signaling indirect discourse, the change of pronouns and verb tense makes it clear that Agassiz is referring only to himself.]

PART 5

Effective Sentences and Words

CHAPTER 15

Clarity of Sentence Structure

Readers today often are under time pressure and are not willing to spend valuable minutes trying to decode a piece of writing. Writers should accommodate their readers by making their writing as clear and concise as possible.

CLARITY AND CONCISENESS

There are several techniques that you can use for writing as clearly as possible. These include:

- Avoiding excessively long sentences
- Avoiding unnecessary repetition and redundancy
- Eliminating wordy phrases
- Avoiding a noun-heavy style
- Choosing precise words
- Making comparisons complete and clear

15a Avoid excessively long sentences

Sentences that are more than about twenty-five words long sometimes can be difficult for a reader, especially if the sentences are complicated.

> Despite their significance in contemporary society, social movements seldom solve social problems, because in order to mobilize resources a movement must appeal to a broad constituency, which means that the group must focus on large-scale issues which are deeply embedded in society.

This sentence is forty-two words long. The following three shorter sentences say the same thing and are much easier for the reader to understand:

> Despite their significance in contemporary society, social movements seldom solve social problems. To mobilize resources, a movement must appeal to a broad constituency. This means that the group must focus on large-scale issues which are deeply embedded in society.

15b Avoid unnecessary repetition and redundancy

A certain amount of repetition is necessary, both for emphasis and to maintain focus. Repetition is especially useful for linking one sentence to another. However, unnecessary repetition will only clutter your writing and irritate readers.

Life offers many lessons, ~~about life.~~

Redundancy is the use of words that could be left out without changing the meaning of the sentence. Saying that something is *blue in color* is redundant, because readers already know that blue is a color.

15c Eliminate wordy phrases

Many commonly used phrases are unnecessarily long. If you can replace them with no loss of meaning, you should do so.

~~In a very real sense,~~ ^T^trickle-down economics ~~exhibits a tendency~~ *tends* to trickle up, benefiting only the rich.

Wordy phrases	*Concise phrases*
as a matter of fact	in fact
at the present time	today, presently
at this point in time	now
due to the fact that	because

15d Avoid a noun-heavy style

A noun-heavy style is characterized by many more nouns than verbs. It tends to make excessive use of the verb *be* (*am, are, is, was, were*) and have strings of prepositional phrases.

NOUN-HEAVY   Thomas Jefferson was not a believer in the divinity of Jesus Christ and indeed was the author of a version of the Four Gospels that included the removal of all references to "miraculous" events.

MORE VERBAL   Thomas Jefferson did not believe in the divinity of Jesus Christ and indeed wrote a version of the Four Gospels from which he removed all references to "miraculous" events.

15e Choose words that express your meaning precisely

Good writing conveys its meaning efficiently, with precision. Such precision is achieved largely through the careful selection of words. Minimize your use of vague nouns like *area, aspect, factor, kind, nature, situation, sort, thing,* and *type,* as well as your use of vague adjectives like *bad, good, interesting, nice,* and *weird* and vague adverbs like *basically, completely, definitely, really,* and *very.*

WEBLINK

http://www.wisc.edu/ writing/Handbook/ ClearConciseSentences.html

A resource for writing clear and concise sentences

Democracy

~~A democratic type of government basically~~ requires ~~a pretty~~ *an* informed citizenry.

15f   Make comparisons complete and clear

Comparative constructions inherently involve two terms: "*A* is _____er than *B*.*" In formal writing, you should make both terms of the comparison explicit.

INCOMPLETE   Talk radio has become a popular form of entertainment because it gets people more involved.   [More involved than what?]

COMPLETE   Talk radio has become a popular form of entertainment because it gets people more involved than most other media do.

COORDINATION AND SUBORDINATION

In any piece of writing, readers will instinctively look for the most important points. By emphasizing these points and de-emphasizing others, writers make their main points easier to locate in the text and thereby make their writing more readable.

Two important ways to create emphasis are through coordination and subordination of sentence elements. Remember, *form should reflect content*. If two related ideas are equally important, *coordinate* them by putting them on the same grammatical level. If they are not equally important, put the less important idea in a grammatically *subordinate* form.

15g   Look for a way to combine closely related sentences

Writing that contains one short sentence after another not only is unpleasantly choppy but also fails to emphasize some sentences more than others.

TOO CHOPPY

> I was born and raised in a small midwestern town. It was easy to make friends. I got to know a lot of people. I was able to achieve almost all of my goals. I could do almost anything I wanted to.

This paragraph is so choppy that it is hard to get a sense of what the writer's main point is. You can solve this problem by noticing that several pairs of sentences are closely related and combining these sentences.

REVISED VERSION

> I was born and raised in a small midwestern town. It was easy to make friends, *and so* I got to know a lot of people. *Since* I could do almost anything I wanted to, I was able to achieve almost all of my goals.

15h Coordinate related sentences of equal value

Coordination is the pairing of sentences or sentence elements by putting them in the same grammatical form and linking them via a coordinating conjunction, conjunctive adverb, or semicolon. The coordinating conjunctions include *and, but, or, nor, for, so,* and *yet.*

USE OF A COORDINATING CONJUNCTION

> A high-fiber diet appears to lower the risk of certain cancers, *so* the National Cancer Institute recommends consuming 25–35 grams of fiber a day.

Conjunctive adverbs provide another way of giving equal emphasis to two conjoined sentences. The conjunctive adverbs include *however, consequently, therefore, thus, hence, furthermore, moreover, afterward, indeed,* and *otherwise.* They often are preceded by a semicolon.

USE OF A CONJUNCTIVE ADVERB

> The 1928 Pact of Paris offended nobody, since it included no compulsory machinery of enforcement; *hence,* the European nations rushed to sign it.

A coordinate relationship also can be created between two sentences simply by using a semicolon.

USE OF A SEMICOLON

> People are affected by social forces sometimes far removed from their immediate perceptions; they perceive only a relatively small portion of the influences that play upon them.

15i Subordinate less important ideas

To combine two closely related but unequal ideas, use **subordination;** put the more important idea in a main clause and the lesser one in a subordinate clause. Subordinate clauses are typically set off by subordinating conjunctions (such as *although, because, if, since, though, unless, until,* and *while*) or by relative pronouns (such as *that, which, who, whom,* and *whose*).

USE OF A SUBORDINATING CONJUNCTION

> *Even though* we know that advertisers are "out to get us," we do not make much of an attempt to refute their messages.

> Using hands-on experience is one of the best ways of learning, *as* it helps the student learn on a more interactive level.

USE OF A RELATIVE PRONOUN

> The Great Lakes cool the hot winds of summer and warm the cold winds of winter, *which* gives the state of Michigan a milder climate than some of the other north central states.

PARALLELISM

Whenever a writer links two or more words or phrases that have similar roles in a sentence, readers expect to see them in the same grammatical form. When the linked similar words or phrases are balanced and in the same form, the result is called **parallelism** (or *parallel structure* or *parallel form*). When Benjamin Franklin wrote "A penny saved is a penny earned," he was using parallelism. The adjective *saved* parallels in content and form the adjective *earned*.

Parallelism not only can make writing more elegant; it also can direct the reader's attention to important structural relationships among ideas within sentences. Putting two elements in parallel form makes it easy for the reader to compare them.

15j Put parallel content in parallel form

Words and phrases that are linked by the coordinating conjunctions *and, but, or,* or *nor* often are parallel in content. In such cases, they also should be parallel in form, using the same grammatical structure.

> *cease* and *desist* [Both verbs]
>
> *hook, line,* and *sinker* [All nouns]
>
> *of the people, by the people,* [and] *for the people* [All prepositional phrases]

15k Make all items in a list or series parallel

Whenever you present any kind of listing in formal or academic writing, whether it is a formatted list such as an outline or just a series of items in a sentence, all of the items should be in the same grammatical form.

NONPARALLEL SERIES REVISED

> The last decades of the 19th century through the early decades
>
> of our present century marked a period when Americans
>
> confronted rapid industrialization, a communications revolution,
> *the growth of big business.*
> and ~~big business was growing.~~ [A third noun phrase is put into the series to replace the distracting clause.]

15l Use parallelism with correlative conjunctions

Whenever you use correlative conjunctions such as *both/and, either/or, neither/nor,* or *not only/but,* you are lining up two sentence elements for comparison. Thus, those elements require parallel grammatical form.

> Either *we go full speed ahead* or *we stop right here.*

15m Use parallelism for comparisons or contrasts

A comparison or contrast involves two statements or terms that are seen as somehow equivalent; indeed, it is this equivalence that allows them to be compared. These two statements or terms therefore should be parallel. A good example of contrasting parallelism occurs in Shakespeare's *Julius Caesar*, where Brutus tries to justify, before the citizens of Rome, his assassination of Caesar:

> Not that I loved Caesar less, but that I loved Rome more. Had you rather Caesar were living, and die all slaves, than that Caesar were dead, to live all free men?

> —*Julius Caesar*, 3.2.21–24

VARIETY

Good writers always try to make their writing interesting, not only in content but also in style. This is where variety comes in. By varying your style, you change the rhythm of your writing and keep your readers interested. If you write the same kind of sentence over and over again, you are likely to put your readers to sleep.

15n Vary sentence length

One of the easiest and most effective ways to alter the rhythm of your writing is to vary the length of your sentences. You do not have to change length with every sentence, but you certainly should do so from time to time. Note how Barbara Kingsolver does it in the opening paragraph of *The Bean Trees*:

> I have been afraid of putting air in a tire ever since I saw a tractor tire blow up and throw Newt Hardbine's father over the top of the Standard Oil sign. I'm not lying. He got stuck up there. About nineteen people congregated during the time it took for Norman Strick to walk up to the Courthouse and blow the whistle for the volunteer fire department.

> —Barbara Kingsolver, *The Bean Trees*

15o Vary sentence structure

Another way to alter the rhythm and cadence of your writing is by varying the structure of your sentences. Based on clause structure, sentences can be divided into four basic types:

- A **simple sentence** contains one independent clause and no other clauses.
- A **compound sentence** contains two independent clauses.
- A **complex sentence** contains one independent clause and one or more subordinate clauses.
- A **compound-complex sentence** contains two independent clauses and at least one subordinate clause.

15p Avoid excessive repetition

Repetition always draws attention. If you use it deliberately to create parallelism or emphasis, that is fine. But if you use it for no particular reason, you will only draw attention to your repetitiveness—not a good way to liven up your style!

CHAPTER **16**

Word-Processing Tools and Online Resources

Among the conveniences of using a computer for writing is the ready access to editing and formatting tools, which are found in any standard word-processing program. But these tools must be used with care. This chapter discusses such word-processing tools as style/grammar checkers and style templates. (Thesauruses and dictionaries are discussed in Chapter 23.) The chapter concludes with a brief discussion of the kinds of Internet sites that can be helpful in sentence revision.

16a Use a style/grammar checker only with caution

A typical style/grammar checker will scan your document and apply whatever rules it has been programmed to observe. Since the rules reflected in the programs are taken from traditional grammar and style books, computerized style/grammar checkers are similar in the kinds of things they flag, such as long sentences, archaic words, sexist expressions, double negatives, sentence fragments, and passive verbs.

1 Problems overlooked by style/grammar checkers

Style/grammar checkers can be useful in pointing out potential trouble spots, but they have serious shortcomings. First, they overlook many potential problems. Of all the stylistic and grammatical problems illustrated in the examples in Part 4 of this book, for example, our style/grammar checker could identify only a third. It was unable to identify any of the pronoun reference problems in Chapter 10, or any of the modifier problems in Chapter 13, or any of the consistency problems in Chapter 14.

2 Nonconstructive suggestions made by style/grammar checkers

Style/grammar checkers flag many things that are not problematic. In some cases, the computer misreads the sentence. In other cases, it applies a rule too simplistically. For example, if your style/grammar checker flags a passive-voice verb, you may decide that you should change it to active voice. But using the passive voice is not always wrong; indeed, sometimes it is the best choice. Many stylistic choices depend on things that a computer cannot assess.

16b Use style templates

Style templates are preset formats for common types of documents, such as business letters, memos, résumés, and reports. Whenever you need to write these types of documents, you can get off to a quick start by just opening the template (usually in the FILE menu).

Style templates are handy tools, especially if you frequently write the same kind of document. But do not hesitate to modify any template that is preset in your computer.

16c Use other applications for sentence revision

In addition to style/grammar checkers and style templates, word processors offer a number of special functions that can be used in revising sentences or paragraphs. For example, a revisions program allows you to insert changes in a draft and then compare what the draft looks like with and without the changes.

One of the most useful word-processing features is the SEARCH, or FIND, feature (often located in the EDIT menu). This feature can allow you to specify the context in which you want to find a specific word or letter combination.

16d Consult Internet resources for writing help

Chapters 1, 2, and 4 describe how to use the Internet and networking resources for research and for peer exchanges or collaborative work associated with the composition process. In addition, the Internet can provide you with help in writing and revising sentences and in developing stronger word usage. Some of this help can come from useful and entertaining Web sites that offer advice on all kinds of grammar, usage, and vocabulary topics (see the Weblink boxes found throughout this book).

CHAPTER **17**

Choosing the Right Words and Avoiding Biased Language

Since meaning is conveyed through words, a writer's choice of words, or **diction,** is crucial. Choose your words carefully, and you will make your writing clearer and more interesting; choose your words carelessly, and you may leave your readers frustrated.

Writers sometimes use the power of language negatively to express bias, the one-sided (usually negative) characterization of an entire group. Writers should try at all times to avoid bias in their writing.

17a Choose the right denotation

The **denotation** of a word is its basic dictionary meaning. The verbs *walk, stroll, hobble, saunter, promenade, hike, march,* and *tramp* all have the same basic meaning, or denotation—"to move by alternately putting one foot in front of the other, always having at least one foot on the ground." Unlike these words, the verbs *run, walk,* and *crawl* differ in denotation. Your first obligation in choosing words is to select ones that accurately denote whatever idea you are trying to convey. For example, if Julie *crawled* to the nearest house, it would be a misrepresentation to say that she either *walked* or *ran.*

1 General statements versus specific details

All good writing involves a mixture of general statements and specific details. General statements establish main points, while specific details make these points precise, vivid, and memorable. Good writers thus continually make choices among words whose denotations range from general to specific. For example, instead of deciding whether Julie *ran, walked,* or *crawled,* the writer could have chosen to use a verb with a more general meaning, such as *go.*

2 Abstract versus concrete nouns

Abstract nouns are those that have broad, often vague denotations, like *power,* *romance,* and *democracy.* Such words refer to concepts rather than to tangible objects. **Concrete nouns** refer to things that are available to the senses—things that we can see, touch, hear, smell, or taste. For example, *raccoon, Statue of Liberty,* and *radishes* all bring to mind tangible, concrete objects. As with general statements and specific details, you should aim for a mixture of the abstract and the concrete.

17b Choose the right connotation

Connotations are the extra nuances of meaning that distinguish otherwise synonymous words. *Walk, stroll, hobble, saunter, promenade, hike, march,* and *tramp* all are considered synonyms, yet each brings to mind a somewhat different image. Make sure that you are aware of a word's connotations before you use the word; otherwise, the message you convey to your readers may be very different from the one you intended.

WEBLINK

http://www.uottawa.ca/
academic/arts/writcent/
hypergrammar/diction.html

A hyperlinked discussion of
denotation, connotation,
catch phrases, and clichés

17c Find the right level of formality

Words vary in their level of formality, or register, from very formal to colloquial. Always listen to what you are writing, to make sure that you consistently use words in the appropriate register.

1 Formal, academic vocabulary

Virtually all writing you do for school and college assignments (except for special cases such as creative writing or personal narratives) should be in a fairly formal register, as is this handbook. Formal, academic vocabulary consists largely of words derived from Latin and Greek—words like *inevitable, hypothesis, perception, theory,* and *superfluous*—which is why you are tested on such words when you take the SAT and ACT exam.

2 Informal vocabulary

Informal words are those you might use in ordinary, everyday contexts such as talking with friends and sending email messages.

Although informal vocabulary is sometimes acceptable in formal writing, you should generally try to use the more formal equivalents where possible.

Informal	Formal	Informal	Formal
friendly	amicable	do again	repeat
worn out	exhausted	go faster	accelerate

17d Avoid jargon, slang, or dialect

There are many versions of English, only one of which—Standard Edited English—is represented in this book. Standard Edited English is the version most widely used in academic and professional contexts and most widely understood around the world. Other versions, including jargon, slang, and dialect, are valuable in their own right. However, they are less widely understood, and thus you should refrain from using them except with audiences composed of fellow "insiders."

Jargon is any technical language used by professionals, sports enthusiasts, hobbyists, or other special-interest groups. By naming objects and concepts that are unique to a group's special interests, jargon facilitates communication among members of the group.

Used by teenagers and other subcultures, slang is a deliberately colorful form of speech, whose appeal depends on novelty and freshness. For this reason, slang terms tend to be short-lived, quickly giving way to newer, fresher replacements.

A dialect is the type of speech used by a specific social, ethnic, or regional group. Dialects typically have a distinctive accent, many unique words and expressions, and even some grammatical patterns that differ from those of Standard Edited English.

17e Avoid pretentiousness

College students are continually exposed to the discourse of academics—professors, scholars, textbook writers—who have spent most of their adult lives developing a large vocabulary and an embellished style of writing. If you find yourself tempted to imitate this style of discourse, do so with great caution. You are at risk of sounding pretentious.

17f Use figurative language

Figurative language uses words in nonliteral, creative ways to enhance the reader's understanding. Two of the most common figures of speech are **simile** and **metaphor,** both of which attempt to explain the unfamiliar by comparing it to the familiar.

When they are still fresh, metaphors add sparkle to writing. But over time, if they are used heavily, they become worn out and lose their charm. An overused metaphor is called a *cliché*. Some examples of clichés are *white as a sheet, barking up the wrong tree,* and *climbing the ladder of success*. Good writers avoid clichés in formal writing.

17g Avoid biased gender references

In the past, men and women had distinctly different roles in society. Language developed accordingly. A doctor was presumed to be male; in the relatively few cases where a doctor happened to be a woman, she was referred to as a *woman doctor*. A nurse, on the other hand, was presumed to be female; gender was indicated only in those relatively few cases involving a *male nurse*.

Stereotyping can arise unwittingly through the careless use of examples and illustrations. Try to vary the roles of men and women in your examples, thereby broadening the spectrum of possibilities for both sexes.

> **WEBLINK**
>
> http://owl.english.purdue
> .edu/handouts/general/
> gl_nonsex.html
>
> Guidelines for nonsexist
> language from the Purdue
> Online Writing Lab

1 Gender-specific nouns

In general, do not use gender-marked terms in situations where a person's gender should not be of any relevance.

Sexist	*Gender-neutral*
businessmen	businesspersons
foremen	supervisors
manpower	personnel, staff

2 Generic pronouns

Traditionally, *he, him,* and *his* were used as **generic pronouns** to refer to all members of a group, regardless of sex. A sentence such as "Everyone should pay attention to his spelling" would supposedly apply to both males and females. But using only masculine words as generic pronouns has been found to be discriminatory in its psychological effects.

17h Avoid biased language about race and ethnicity

Language that either intentionally or unintentionally discriminates against people because of their race or ethnicity is a form of verbal aggression. Unbiased writers reject the sort of disparaging stereotyping evident in ethnic jokes and in sweeping statements about ethnic groups.

17i Avoid biased language about age and other differences

In our youth-oriented culture, it is not uncommon to hear demeaning references to age. Indeed, the adjective *old* often is used gratuitously as a way of denigrating others. Avoid age-related stereotypes and expressions in examples and jokes.

Occupational, religious, political, regional, socioeconomic, and disability-related groups are among the many other groupings in our society that are subject to stereotyping. As with ethnic groups, it is generally best to refer to such groups in ways that they themselves prefer. For example, most people with physical disabilities prefer to be called *physically disabled* rather than *handicapped,* and most people who clean buildings prefer the title of *custodian* rather than that of *janitor.* Such preferences should be respected.

CHAPTER **18**

End Punctuation

There are three ways to punctuate the end of a sentence: with a period, a question mark, or an exclamation point.

THE PERIOD

The period is used to indicate the end of a statement, to punctuate initials and abbreviations, and to mark basic divisions in units and computer names.

WEBLINK

http://www.uottawa.ca/
academic/arts/writcent/
hypergrammar/endpunct
.html

All about end punctuation

18a Use a period to mark the end of a statement

Sometimes called a "full stop," the period is most commonly used to mark the end of a sentence. Just make sure before you place the period that the words form a *complete grammatical sentence*, or else you will be creating a sentence fragment (see Chapter 11).

18b Use periods to punctuate initials, abbreviations, unit divisions, and computer names

Initials that stand for middle names or first names take periods:

Mary W. Shelley   O. J. Simpson   F. Scott Fitzgerald

Leave one space after each period when punctuating initials in names. Most abbreviations ending in lowercase letters take periods.

Ms.   St.   Jan.
Dr.   apt.   Inc.

Basic divisions in money, measurements, email addresses, and file names all take periods:

$99.50   3.2 meters   13.5 gallons
English.paper.doc   michael.okiwara@u.cc.utah.edu

18c Avoid common misuses of periods

WEBLINK

http://stipo.larc.nasa.gov/
sp7084/sp7084ch3.html
A description of all uses of
the period and the question
mark

1. *Do not use a period to mark just any pause.* If you insert a period whenever you want readers to pause, you run the risk of creating sentence fragments. Consider this example:

Attempts to challenge reactionary political views are often branded as "politically correct" by those same reactionaries. *Who support only their own versions of "free speech."*
[The second sentence is a fragment.]

2. *Do not use periods with acronyms and other all uppercase abbreviations.*

CA	NJ	USA	UN	FBI
NOW	NAACP	MS-DOS	CD-ROM	COBOL

3. *Do not use periods at the end of stand-alone titles or headings.* The title of this chapter and its numbered headings are examples of stand-alone titles and headings, respectively.

4. *Do not use periods at the end of sentences within sentences.*

   The famous statement "I think, therefore I am" originated in an essay by the French philosopher Descartes.

5. *Do not use periods after items in a formatted list (except for full sentences).* The table of contents for this handbook is an example of a formatted list. Only when the items in the list are full sentences is it acceptable to have periods after the individual items.

THE QUESTION MARK

Question marks are placed after direct questions, whereas periods follow indirect questions. Do not use a comma or a period after a question mark.

18d Use a question mark after a direct request

REQUESTING INFORMATION	Who wrote *Jesus Christ, Superstar* ?
ASKING FOR CONFIRMATION	It's a complicated situation, isn't it ?
MAKING A POLITE REQUEST	Could you please be a little quieter ?

1 Using question marks with direct and indirect quotations

If the direct quotation is a question and it is at the end of the sentence, put the question mark inside the quotation marks.

The police officer asked me, "Do you live here ?"

Do not use a question mark after an indirect question. An indirect question is the writer's rewording of a question posed by someone else.

A tourist asked me where the Lincoln Memorial was.

2 Using question marks in a series

It is acceptable to put a question mark after each independent item in a series, even if it is not a full sentence.

> Will our homeless population continue to grow**?** Stay about the same**?** Get smaller**?**

If the question is an either/or type, put a question mark only at the end of the sentence.

> Are you coming with us or staying here**?**

THE EXCLAMATION POINT

Exclamation points are used to show strong emotion, including amazement and sarcasm. Do not use a comma or a period after an exclamation point.

18e   **Use an exclamation point to signal a strong statement**

The statement marked with an exclamation point does not have to be a full sentence.

AN OUTCRY OR COMMAND	Oh**!** Watch out**!**
STRONG EMPHASIS	People before profits**!**
ASTONISHMENT	Imagine reading this news report and not getting upset**!**
SARCASM	And the cigarette companies claim that smoking is not addictive**!**

CHAPTER 19

The Comma, Semicolon, and Colon

Three of the most common and most useful punctuation marks in the English language—and also the most difficult to master—are the comma, semicolon, and colon. This chapter provides some guidelines (not rules) for the use of these punctuation marks.

THE COMMA

One way to show a close relationship between independent clauses is with a comma.

19a   Use a comma to set off an introductory phrase or clause

When readers start to read a sentence, one of the first things they do (unconsciously) is try to locate the grammatical subject. Help them do this by setting off with a comma any potentially distracting words that *precede* the subject.

Using a comma after an introductory element is especially important in cases where it is needed to prevent possible confusion.

> **WEBLINK**
>
> http://owl.english.purdue
> .edu/handouts/grammar/
> g_comma.html
> A discussion of the main uses
> of the comma, accompanied
> by good proofreading
> strategies and exercises

CONFUSING   Soon after starting the car began making funny noises.

CLEAR   Soon after starting, the car began making funny noises.

19b Use a comma before a coordinating conjunction to separate independent clauses

The combination of a comma and a coordinating conjunction (*and, but, or, nor, for, so, yet*) is one of the most common ways of connecting independent clauses.

> Members of a mainstream culture often feel threatened by a counterculture**, *and*** they sometimes move against it in the attempt to affirm their own values.

When you are using a coordinating conjunction to link phrases rather than clauses, you generally do not insert a comma.

> Acupuncture has proved effective for treating chronic pain∕and for blocking acute pain briefly.   [The simple parallel phrases need no separation; a revision removes the unnecessary comma.]

However, writers sometimes insert a comma to create more separation between the two parts.

> Acupressure is similar to acupuncture¸but does not use needles.   [The contrastive phrase is separated with a comma.]

19c Use commas between items in a series

A series of three or more items should have commas after all but the last item.

> My super-patriotic neighbor says *red**,** white**,** and blue* are his favorite colors.

Occasionally in journalistic writing or in company names composed of three or more personal names, the last comma in the series—called the **serial comma**—is omitted.

> My uncle used to work for *Pierce, Fenner and Smith.*

19d　Use commas to separate coordinate adjectives

When the adjectives in a series could be arranged in any order or could be (but are not) strung together with the use of *and*, they are termed **coordinate adjectives**. To show their loose relationship and also to avoid confusion with adjectives that cumulate in a particular order to modify each other, separate coordinate adjectives with commas.

> A *rusty, dented, broken-down* car was left behind.

In this example, each adjective modifies the word *car*.

19e　Use commas to set off nonessential phrases or clauses

A nonessential element, or **nonrestrictive element**, provides an extra piece of information that can be left out without changing the basic meaning of the sentence. Always use punctuation to set off nonessential, or nonrestrictive, elements from the rest of the sentence. (By contrast, elements that are essential, or restrictive, are always integrated into the sentence without separating punctuation.) Nonessential elements are most commonly set off with commas; however, parentheses or dashes may also be used.

> Lung cancer, *the leading cause of cancer deaths in the United States,* kills more than 153,000 Americans each year.　[A nonessential appositive is set off with commas.]

Unless the nonessential element ends the sentence, be sure to use *two* commas to set it off, not just one.

19f　Use commas to set off conjunctive adverbs

Conjunctive adverbs include the words and phrases *however, therefore, consequently, thus, furthermore, on the other hand, in general*, and *in other words*. They serve as useful transitional devices, helping the reader to follow the flow of the writer's thinking. By enclosing conjunctive adverbs in commas, you give them more prominence, clearly marking a shift in thinking.

> Resistance training exercises cause microscopic damage to muscle fibers, which take twenty-four to forty-eight hours to heal; *therefore,* resistance training programs require at least one day of rest between workouts.

19g Use commas with dates, place names and addresses, titles and degrees, and numbers

When writing a date in the traditional American format of month, day, and year, set off the year by placing a comma after the day.

> John F. Kennedy died on November 22, 1963.

Do not use a comma if only the month and year are given.

> John F. Kennedy died in November 1963.

Use commas after all major elements in a place name or address. However, do not put a comma before a zip code.

> Aretha Franklin was born in Memphis, Tennessee, on March 25, 1942.
> Alfredo's new address is 112 Ivy Lane, Englewood, NJ 07631.

Use commas to set off a title or degree following a person's name.

> Stella Martinez, MD, was the attending physician.

Use a comma in numbers of five digits or more, to form three-digit groups. In a number of four digits, the comma is optional.

> 2,400 OR 2400
> 56,397
> 1,000,000

Exceptions: Do not use commas in street numbers, zip codes, telephone numbers, account numbers, model numbers, or years.

19h Use commas with speaker tags

If you are quoting someone and using a speaker tag (such as *he said, according to Freud,* or *notes Laurel Stuart*), put a comma between the tag and the quotation.

> *Thomas Edison said,* "Genius is 1 percent inspiration and 99 percent perspiration."

19i Use commas with markers of direct address

Put commas around words that indicate that you are talking directly to the reader: words such as *yes* or *no*, the reader's name (*Bob*), question tags (*don't you agree?*), or mild initiators (*Well, Oh*).

> *Yes,* the stock market is likely to turn around.

> Do you really think, *Grace,* that Professor Wilson will postpone the test?

19j Avoid misuse of commas

1. *Never use a single comma between the subject and predicate.* When a complex subject begins a sentence, writers sometimes feel inclined to add an inappropriate comma that splits the subject and predicate.

FAULTY COMMA REVISED

> Numerous psychological and social factors∕have a strong influence on how people age.

2. *Never use commas with restrictive elements.* **Restrictive elements** are phrases or clauses that are essential to defining the meaning of the sentence. They should not be set off with commas.

> Consumers∕who are considering using a hospital or clinic∕should scrutinize the facility's accreditation.   [In this sentence, the writer is referring not to all consumers but only to those who are considering using a hospital or clinic.]

3. *Avoid using commas with cumulative adjectives.* Adjectives that accumulate before a noun, each one modifying those that follow, are called **cumulative adjectives**. Their modifying relationships, which depend on their order, are likely to be confused by the separating commas that are common with adjectives in a coordinate series.

CONFUSING COMMAS REVISED

The suspect was seen driving a *small/ new/ Italian/ luxury/* car.

4. *Avoid putting a comma before* than. Resist the urge to heighten a comparison or contrast by using commas to separate the *than* clause from the rest of the sentence.

FAULTY COMMA REVISED

Beating our arch-rival was more important/ than getting to the state playoffs.

5. *Avoid using a comma after a subordinating conjunction.* A comma should not be used to separate a subordinating conjunction from its own clause; it should be used before the conjunction to separate the entire clause from the rest of the sentence.

FAULTY COMMA REVISED

Although/ the car is fifteen years old, it seems to be in good shape.

6. *Never use a comma before parentheses or after a question mark or exclamation point.* A comma is superfluous with an opening parenthesis, question mark, or exclamation point.

UNNECESSARY COMMAS REVISED

Muhammad was born in Mecca/ (now in Saudi Arabia) and founded the religion of Islam around AD 610.

7. *Do not insert a comma before a list.* Resist the urge to punctuate before a listed series.

UNNECESSARY COMMAS REVISED

Some countries, such as,/Holland, Sweden, and Denmark, have very compassionate welfare systems.

8. *Do not use a comma in a two-item series.* While commas are needed to separate three or more items in series, separating two items with a comma is unnecessary and distracting.

UNNECESSARY COMMA REVISED

Her outfit used strong contrasts between red,/and blue.

THE SEMICOLON

A semicolon is used mainly when two clauses have a coordinate relationship—that is, when they convey equally important ideas (see 15h) but do not have a coordinating conjunction (*and, but, or, not, for, so, yet*) between them.

19k	Use a semicolon to separate independent clauses not linked by a coordinating conjunction

When there is no coordinating conjunction, related independent clauses should be connected with a semicolon rather than a comma.

The first panacea for a mismanaged nation is inflation of the currency; the second is war. Both bring a temporary prosperity; both bring a permanent ruin.

—Ernest Herningway, *Notes on the Next War*

WEBLINK

http://web.wisc.edu/ writing/Handbook/ Semicolons.html

A complete guide to semicolons

19l Use a semicolon to separate independent clauses linked by a conjunctive adverb

If you separate two independent clauses with a conjunctive adverb such as *however*, *therefore*, or *nevertheless*, you must use a semicolon.

> More than 185 countries belong to the United Nations; *however*, only five of them have veto power.

19m Use semicolons in a series with internal punctuation

A **complex series** is one that has internal punctuation. Normally, commas are used to separate items in a series; however, if the individual items contain commas, it can be difficult for readers to determine which commas are internal to the items and which commas separate the items. In these cases, semicolons are used to separate the items.

> I have lived in Boulder, Colorado; Corpus Christi, Texas; and Vero Beach, Florida.

19n Place semicolons outside quotation marks

Semicolons are always positioned outside quotation marks.

> Those who feel abortion is not a woman's prerogative say they are "pro-life"; those who feel it is say they are "pro-choice."

19o Avoid common semicolon errors

1. *Do not use a semicolon between an independent clause and a dependent clause or phrase.* Dependent clauses or phrases are linked to independent clauses most often by commas, not semicolons.

> When we say that a country is "underdeveloped"; we imply that it is
> backward in some way.   [The introductory clause should be linked by a comma, not a semicolon.]

2. *Do not use a semicolon to introduce a list.* Use a colon instead.

Utah has five national parks⁏Arches, Bryce, Canyonlands, Capitol
Reef, and Zion.

THE COLON

In formal writing, the colon is used mainly after a general statement to announce details related in some way to the statement. These details may be a
list of items, a quotation, an appositive, or an explanatory statement.

19p　Use a colon to introduce a list or appositive

In using a colon to introduce a list or appositive, be sure that the introductory part of
the sentence is a grammatically complete
clause.

> In creating a macro, you can assign it to
> any one of three places: the toolbar, the
> keyboard, or a menu.

WEBLINK

http://www.uottawa.ca/
academic/arts/writcent/
hypergrammar/colon.html

An introduction to using
the colon

19q　Use a colon to set off a second independent clause that explains the first

> Rock climbing is like vertical chess: in making each move up the wall, you
> should have a broad strategy in mind.

Note: You may begin the clause after the colon with either an uppercase letter
or a lowercase letter.

Although both the colon and the semicolon can be used to separate independent clauses, they cannot be used interchangeably. A semicolon is used
when the two clauses are balanced; a colon is used when the second clause is
a specification of the first.

COLON   Blessed are the pure in heart: for they shall see God.

SEMICOLON   And the earth was without form and void; and darkness was
upon the face of the deep.

19r Use a colon to introduce a quotation

When a colon is used to introduce a quotation, the part of the sentence that
precedes the colon should be grammatically independent.

In *Against Empire*, Michael Parenti states his concern about American
foreign policy: "We should pay less attention to what US policymakers
profess as their motives—for anyone can avouch dedication to noble
causes—and give more attention to what they actually do."

19s Use colons in titles

Colons are often used in the titles of academic papers and reports. The part of
the title that follows the colon is called the subtitle. It usually provides a more
explicit description of the topic than does the title.

Nature and the Poetic Imagination: Death and Rebirth in "Ode to
the West Wind"

19t Use colons in business letters and memos

In business letters and memos, colons are used in salutations (*Dear Ms.
Townsend:*), to separate the writer's initials from the typist's initials (*TH:ab*),
and in memo headings (*To:, From:, Date:, Subject:, Dist:*).

19u Use colons in numbers and addresses

Colons are used in Biblical citations to distinguish chapter from verse
(*Matthew 4:11, Genesis 3:9*), in clock times to separate hours from minutes and
minutes from seconds (*5:44 p.m.*), in ratios (*3:1*), and in Web site addresses
(*http://www.fray.com*).

CHAPTER 20

The Apostrophe and Quotation Marks

THE APOSTROPHE

The apostrophe is used to indicate possession, to alert the reader to contractions and omitted letters, and to form certain plurals.

20a Use apostrophes with nouns to indicate possession

In its grammatical sense, *possession* refers to ownership, amounts, or some other special relationship between two nouns. With singular nouns, possession is usually indicated by attaching 's to the end of the noun.

> Sue Ellen's jacket   yesterday's bad weather

There are two exceptions to this rule:

1. If the rule would lead to awkward pronunciation, the extra s may be omitted: *Euripides' plays, Moses' laws, Mister Rogers' Neighborhood.*
2. In names of places, companies, and institutions, the apostrophe is often omitted: *Robbers Roost, Kings County, Starbucks, Peoples Republic.*

WEBLINK

http://www.grammarbook
.com/punctuation/apostro
.html

An excellent guide to
apostrophes, including
exercises

For plural nouns ending in s, form the possessive by just adding an apostrophe at the end:

> the Browns' car   the Yankees' star pitcher   my parents' friends

For plural nouns not ending in s, form the possessive by adding 's:

> women's rights   children's section   sheep's wool

1 Avoiding apostrophes with possessive pronouns

Pronouns never take apostrophes to indicate possession. They have their own possessive forms: *its, his, her/hers, your/yours, their/theirs, our/ours, my/mine*.

Be careful not to confuse *its* and *it's*. The former is possessive; the latter is a contraction for *it is*.

2 Showing possession with multiple nouns

With multiple nouns, use apostrophes according to your intended meaning. If you want to indicate joint possession, add an apostrophe only to the last of the nouns:

Bush and Cheney's campaign

If you want to show *separate* possession, put an apostrophe after each of the nouns:

Omar's, Gretchen's, and Mike's birthdays

20b Use apostrophes to indicate contractions and omitted letters

In casual speech, syllables are sometimes omitted from common word combinations. For example, *cannot* becomes *can't*. In formal writing, such **contractions** are generally inappropriate. In much informal writing, however, such as email messages and personal letters, contractions are quite common. Just be sure to punctuate them correctly with an apostrophe.

will not → won't	should not → shouldn't	it is → it's
I am → I'm	you have → you've	they are → they're

20c Use apostrophes to mark certain plural forms

When a letter or symbol is used as a noun, the usual way of pluralizing nouns (adding an *s* or *es*) does not work well: "There are four *ss* in *sassafras*." In such cases, an apostrophe can help out.

There are four *s*'s in *sassafras*.

Both the Modern Language Association and the American Psychological Association recommend omitting the apostrophe in forming plurals like the following:

the 1990s   several IOUs   a shipment of PCs

QUOTATION MARKS

The primary use of quotation marks is to acknowledge other people's words and statements. Using quotation marks is especially important in academic writing, which puts a premium on the ownership of ideas.

20d Use quotation marks for exact direct quotations

Quotation marks should be placed around any words, phrases, or sentences that you have borrowed from someone else (unless the quotations are so lengthy that you prefer to set them off as an indented block).

> In *The End of Work*, Jeremy Rifkin said, "In the years ahead, more than 90 million jobs in a labor force of 124 million are potentially vulnerable to replacement by machines."

1 Paraphrasing or quoting indirectly

A summarization, restatement, or paraphrase of a statement made by someone else is a form of **indirect discourse,** and quotation marks are not used. Putting quotation marks around words that were not those of the speaker or writer would be extremely misleading.

MISLEADING QUOTATION MARKS REVISED

> Rifkin argues that "in the future more than two-thirds of the American workforce could be displaced by automation."

2 Setting off long quotations in block form

A long quotation (more than about four lines) should be set off as an indented block without quotation marks.

Rifkin sees this reduction of the workforce as having profound social effects:

The wholesale substitution of machines for workers is going to force every nation to rethink the role of human beings in the social process. Redefining opportunities and responsibilities for millions of people in a society absent of mass formal employment is likely to be the single most pressing social issue of the coming century.

20e Use quotation marks to suggest skepticism about a term

Sometimes you may find yourself writing about a concept that you think does not deserve the respect other people are giving it. In such cases, you can convey your skepticism by putting the name of the concept in quotation marks.

Although many people consider the family the foundation of American society and talk about a return to "family values" as a desirable objective, it is clear that the modern American family looks quite different from families of previous generations.

20f Use quotation marks to indicate shifts of register

Quotation marks can be used occasionally to set off a colloquial term from the more formal discourse surrounding it.

One should always try to avoid an inflexible, "cookie-cutter" approach to rhetorical criticism.

20g Use quotation marks when citing titles of short works

When referring by title to short stories, book chapters, poems, essays, songs, and other brief works, enclose the titles in quotation marks.

"Smells Like Teen Spirit" is a '90s classic.

20h Follow standard practice in using other punctuation with quotations

1. *Put commas and periods inside the end quotation mark.* Standard American editorial practice calls for commas and periods to be placed as shown in the following passage:

"The definition of community implicit in the market model," argues Patricia Hill Collins, "sees community as arbitrary and fragile, structured fundamentally by competition and domination."

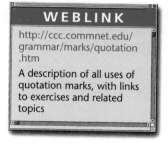

WEBLINK

http://ccc.commnet.edu/
grammar/marks/quotation
.htm

A description of all uses of quotation marks, with links to exercises and related topics

2. *Put colons and semicolons outside the end quotation mark.*

One critic called 1990 "the year in which rock & roll was reborn": the fusing of metal and rap by groups like Living Colour and Faith No More broke down racial barriers in a way reminiscent of early rock & roll.

3. *Put other punctuation marks inside the end quotation mark if they are part of the quotation; otherwise, put them outside the end quotation mark.* Question marks, exclamation points, dashes, parentheses, and other punctuation marks should be positioned according to meaning.

PART OF QUOTED TITLE

Whitney Houston's "How Will I Know?" entered the pop charts at number one.

PART OF SENTENCE

What do you think of controversial songs like "Deep Cover" and "Cop Killer"?

4. *Use single quotation marks (' ') for quotation marks within quotation marks.*

> Garofalo notes that "on cuts like 'JC' and 'Swimsuit Issue,' Sonic Youth combined an overt sexuality with uncompromisingly feminist lyrics about women's issues."

5. *Introduce quotations with the punctuation standard grammar calls for.* The sentence or phrase you use to introduce a quotation should be punctuated according to the grammatical relationship between the introduction and the quotation. If the introduction is not a grammatically complete sentence, do not use any punctuation.

> The conservative Parents Music Resource Center maintained that heavy metal was "the most disturbing element in contemporary music."

CHAPTER 21

Other Punctuation Marks

WEBLINK

http://stipo.larc.nasa.gov/
sp7084/sp7084ch3.html

A full discussion of parentheses, dashes, brackets, ellipses, and slashes

Parentheses, dashes, brackets, ellipses, and slashes can all be used, in moderation and in proper contexts, to clarify meaning and add interest to writing.

PARENTHESES

Parentheses are indispensable to formal writing. Be sure, though, not to overuse them.

21a Use parentheses to insert parenthetical comments

Usually, parenthetical comments—clarifications, asides, examples, or other extra pieces of information—are embedded within sentences. They can be as short as a single word or as long as an entire sentence.

> For most right-handed people, the left hemisphere of the brain controls manual skills and language (and vice versa for most left-handed people).

Another common use of parentheses is in documentation. The scientific reference style calls for inserting reference citations in parentheses within sentences (see Chapters 5 and 6). This parenthetical style is the preferred method of the MLA, APA, and CBE.

21b Do not overuse parentheses

Parentheses are so handy that you may be tempted to overuse them. Resist the temptation. Too many parentheses can make it difficult for readers to follow the main train of thought.

21c Use parentheses around letters or numbers to set off embedded lists

Listed phrases or clauses embedded in a longer sentence may be itemized with numbers or letters placed within parentheses.

> Socialism has three essential components: (1) the public ownership of the means of production, (2) central planning, and (3) distribution of goods without a profit motive.

DASHES

Dashes are an informal kind of punctuation, with several uses and some misuses. You can create a dash either by typing two hyphens, which some word processors will then convert into a solid dash, or by opening the special character or symbol feature of your word-processing program and selecting the full-length dash (called the "em dash").

21d Use dashes to highlight extra informational comments

Dashes set off internal, informational comments in a more emphatic way than parentheses do.

> Public decision makers have a tendency to focus mostly on the more obvious and immediate environmental problems—usually described as "pollution"—rather than on the deterioration of natural ecosystems upon whose continued functioning global civilization depends.

21e Use dashes to set off important or surprising points

If not overused, dashes can be a dramatic way to set off an inserted comment.

> While the Marshall Islanders continue to wrestle with the consequences of nuclear testing, a new proposal is on the table that will make the islands a dumping ground for American garbage—literally.

21f Confine yourself to one pair of dashes per sentence

Dashes, like parentheses, can be overused. If you need to add more than one informational comment to a sentence, use commas or parentheses around the other comments. Too many dashes in a paragraph are a sign of poorly integrated ideas.

BRACKETS

Brackets are an important editorial device for providing proper context for the quoted or cited material used in research writing.

21g   Use brackets to insert editorial comments or clarifications into quotations

Quotations represent someone's exact words. If you choose to alter those words (because of a misspelling in the original quotation or to add explanatory information, for example), you must indicate that you have done so by putting brackets around the alterations.

> "One of the things that will produce a stalemate in Rio [*the site of the 1992 UN conference on the environment*] is the failure of the chief negotiators, from both the north and the south, to recognize the contradictions between the free market and environmental protection."

> **WEBLINK**
>
> http://ccc.commnet.edu/
> grammar/marks/marks.htm
> Excellent coverage of a range
> of punctuation marks from
> the common to the rarely
> used, with illustrations

The Latin word *sic* (meaning "so" or "thus") indicates a mechanical error—for example, an error of grammar, usage, or spelling—in a quotation. Enclose it in brackets.

> "Any government that wants to more and more restrict freedoms will do it by financial means, by creating financial vacums [*sic*]."

21h   Use brackets to acknowledge editorial emphasis within a quotation

When you quote a passage, you may want to emphasize a certain part of it that is not emphasized in the original. You can do so by underlining or italicizing that part and then, at the end of the passage, acknowledging the change by writing *emphasis added* or *italics mine* between brackets.

21i Use brackets for parenthetical comments within parentheses

If one parenthetical comment is nested within another, punctuate the inner one with brackets to distinguish it from the outer one.

> The spectacular palace that King Louis XIV built at Versailles (which is located 19 kilometers [12 miles] west of Paris) required 35,000 workers and 27 years to construct.

ELLIPSES

An ellipsis (plural: ellipses) is a series of three periods, used to indicate a deletion from a quotation or a pause in a sentence. An ellipsis consists of three *spaced* periods (. . .), not three bunched ones (...). If you end a quoted sentence with an ellipsis, use a fourth period to indicate the end of the sentence.

> "The notion of literature as a secular scripture extends roughly from Matthew Arnold to Northrop Frye. . . ."

The *MLA Handbook for Writers of Research Papers*, 6th edition, notes that some instructors advocate placing brackets around any ellipses points you insert in a quoted passage. However, it prefers using brackets only to distinguish your own omissions from those of the quoted author.

21j Use an ellipsis to indicate a deletion from a quotation

The sentence with an ellipsis should not be significantly different in meaning from the original sentence, nor should it be ungrammatical.

> "Practically any region on earth will harbor some insect
>
> species—native or exotic—that are functioning near the limits
>
> of their temperature or moisture tolerance."

An ellipsis can be used to mark a deletion from either the middle or the end of a sentence, but not the beginning of a sentence.

21k   Use an ellipsis to indicate a pause in a sentence

To mark a pause for dramatic emphasis in your own writing, use an ellipsis.

> I was ready to trash the whole thing ... but then I thought better of it.

SLASHES

Slashes serve a variety of purposes in both formal and informal writing.

21l   Use slashes to separate lines of poetry quoted within a sentence

If you are quoting lines of poetry without setting them off in separate lines as they appear in the poem, put a slash (surrounded by spaces) between the lines.

> Gerard Manley Hopkins's poetry features what he called "sprung rhythms," as can be heard in these lines from "The Windhover": "No wonder of it: sheer plod makes plow down sillion / Shine, and blue-bleak embers, ah my dear, / Fall, gall themselves, and gash gold-vermilion."

21m   Use a slash to show alternatives and to indicate a fraction

Slashes are used in expressions like *either/or, pass/fail, on/off, win/win,* and *writer/editor.* Readers may object, though, if you overuse them. The expressions *he/she, his/her,* and *s/he* are admirable attempts at gender neutrality, but many people dislike their phonetic clumsiness. We suggest you use *he or she* and *his or her* or find other ways of avoiding sexist pronouns.

Fractions that would be set in formal mathematics on separate lines also can be shown on one line, with a slash dividing the numerator from the denominator:

1/3   3/8   2-2/5

21n Use slashes in Internet addresses and informal dates

Slashes are indispensable components of URLs (Web site addresses) like *http://www.ablongman.com/compsite/*. Include the last slash if it brackets a directory, but not if it brackets an actual HTML file.

CHAPTER **22**

Capital Letters, Italics, Abbreviations, and Numbers

CAPITAL LETTERS

Capital (uppercase) letters are used to indicate the start of a new sentence. They also are used for proper names, proper adjectives, and some abbreviations.

22a Capitalize the first word of all free-standing sentences

WEBLINK

http://stipo.larc.nasa.gov/
sp7084/sp7084ch4.html

A discussion of almost all
uses of capital letters

Sentences like the one you are now reading should always start with a capital letter. Sentences that are embedded in other sentences, however, may or may not start with a capital letter, depending on the situation.

If a sentence occurs in parentheses within another sentence, the first word of the parenthetical sentence should not be capitalized:

Major league baseball no longer seems to enjoy the civic loyalty it

for
used to (~~For~~ example, several teams have threatened to leave their cities if new facilities are not built).

If a sentence occurs as a quotation within another sentence and is set off by a colon, comma, or dash, the first word should be capitalized:

Vegetarians
Rush Limbaugh once said, "~~vegetarians~~ are a bunch of weaklings who wouldn't be able to bench press 50 pounds after one of their meals."

However, if the quotation is not set off by a colon, comma, or dash, the first word should be lowercase:

vegetarians
Rush Limbaugh once said that "~~Vegetarians~~ are a bunch of weaklings who wouldn't be able to bench press 50 pounds after one of their meals."

Question fragments can also be capitalized.

Will the stock market keep booming? Level off? Take a dive?

If you are quoting a poem, capitalize the first letter of each line (if the original did so).

> Long as the heart beats life within her breast
>   Thy child will bless thee, guardian mother mild,
> And far away thy memory will be blest
>   By children of the children of thy child.

—Alfred, Lord Tennyson, 1864

22b   Capitalize all names, associated titles, and proper adjectives

Capitalize the first letter of any name, title, or proper adjective referring to a particular person, place, or thing.

1. *Capitalize names and associated titles of people.*

   Ruth Bader Ginsburg   Dr. Harris

   Professor Mixco   Dale Earnhardt, Jr.

2. *Capitalize place names.*

   San Diego, California   the Rockies

   Lake Michigan   Maple Street

Note: Compass points (north, southwest) are capitalized only when they are incorporated into a name (North Carolina) or when they function as nouns denoting a particular region (the Southwest).

3. *Capitalize the names of historic events.*

   World War II   the Middle Ages

   Reconstruction   the My Lai Massacre

4. *Capitalize the names of days, months, holidays, and eras.*

   Monday   the Reagan Era

   April   Thanksgiving

Note: Seasons of the year usually are not capitalized:

   last fall   winter sports   spring semester

5. *Capitalize the names of organizations, companies, and institutions.*

   Common Cause   Intel Corporation

   the United Nations   Alameda Community College

6. *Capitalize the names of products and unique objects.* In most cases, only the first letter of each word in an object or product name is capitalized:

   the Hope Diamond   the North Star

   the *Titanic*   the Boeing 767

Some manufacturers, however, especially in the computer industry, use inter-caps (internal caps):

WordPerfect	QuarkXPress
HotJava	GlobalFax

7. *Capitalize religious, national, and ethnic names.*

Catholicism	Chicano
the Koran	Passover

8. *Capitalize adjectives based on proper nouns.*

American football	Jewish literature
French history	Southern hospitality
Newtonian physics	Islamic tradition

22c Capitalize all significant words in titles

In titles of books, poems, articles, plays, films, and other cultural works, every word except articles (*a, an, the*), conjunctions, and short prepositions should be capitalized. The first word of the title and of the subtitle should be capitalized, even if it is an article, conjunction, or short preposition.

The Joy Luck Club	"Ode to the West Wind"
Death of a Salesman	"Learning in Context: A Qualitative Study"

22d Follow the owner's preferences in capitalizing email addresses and URLs

Although most of the Internet is not case-sensitive, there are two important reasons for writing email and Internet addresses exactly as the owners do. First, some parts of Net addresses, such as the URL pathnames that follow the first single slash, *are* case-sensitive. Second, some Netizens use uppercase and lowercase letters to make important distinctions in their addresses.

ITALICS

In published documents, *italic* typeface is used for a number of purposes. (*Note:* Although most word processors permit the selection of an italic typeface, many instructors prefer that students use *underlining* instead of italics in their papers, as underlined letters and words stand out more than italicized ones.)

22e Italicize titles of independent creative works

Titles of books, magazines, digital magazines ("e-zines"), newspapers, and other creative products that are independently packaged and distributed to a public audience should be written with italics or underlining. Here are some examples:

WEBLINK

http://ccc.commnet.edu/grammar/italics.htm

A brief guide to using italics and underlining

BOOKS   *The Scarlet Letter* or
             The Scarlet Letter

MAGAZINES   *National Geographic* or National Geographic

E-ZINES   *Salon* or Salon

22f Italicize URLs and email addresses

When writing an Internet or email address in the body of a text, use underlining or italics.

Helpful information about current Congressional legislation can be found at *http://thomas.loc.gov/*. The email address is *thomas@loc.gov*.

22g Italicize names of vehicles

Names of particular vehicles, not types of vehicles, should be underlined or italicized. These include the names of spacecraft, airplanes, ships, and trains.

Voyager 2 or Voyager 2
Spirit of St. Louis or Spirit of St. Louis

22h   Italicize foreign words and phrases

In general, it is best to avoid using foreign words and phrases when writing in English. However, if you need to use a foreign expression (for example, because there is no good English equivalent), write it with underlining or italics and, if possible, provide a brief English explanation.

> My Dutch friends say they like being in a *gezellig* environment, one that has a lot of human warmth.

Foreign words that have become common English words should *not* be italicized or underlined. Here are some examples:

machete (Spanish)	judo (Japanese)
sauerkraut (German)	coffee (Arabic)

22i   Italicize words, letters, and numbers referred to as such

When you write a word, letter, or number so as to talk about it as a word, letter, or number, use underlining or italics.

> Many people misspell the word *misspell*; they write it with only one *s*.

Underlining or italics is also appropriate for a word you are about to define. (Alternatively, boldface type can be used.)

> Before starting up a cliff, rock climbers sometimes like to get *beta*—advice from someone who has already done the climb.

ABBREVIATIONS

Abbreviations include shortened versions of words (*Mr., Rev., fig.*), initialisms formed from the first letters of a series of words (*FBI, NBC, IBM*), and acronyms, or initialisms that are pronounced as words (*OPEC, NASA, RAM*). In formal writing, abbreviations should be used sparingly. If you are not sure that readers will know what a certain abbreviation stands for, spell out the word the first time it is used and put the abbreviation in parentheses right after it:

> The Internet uses a domain name system (DNS) for all its servers worldwide.

22j Abbreviate titles, ranks, and degrees only before or after full names

Title before full name	*Degree or rank after full name*
Dr. Teresa Rivera	Derek Rudick, CPA
Prof. Jamie Smith-Weber	Young-Sook Kim, PhD

When titles or ranks are followed by only a surname, they should be spelled out:

> General Powell   Professor Davis

22k Use abbreviations after numerical dates and times

The following abbreviations are commonly used in writing dates and times:

> 124 BC ("before Christ") OR 124 BCE ("before the common era")
>
> AD 567 (*anno Domini*, or "year of our Lord") OR 567 CE ("common era")
>
> 9:40 a.m. (*ante meridiem*) OR 0940 hrs (military or international twenty-four-hour time)
>
> 4:23 p.m. (*post meridiem*) OR 1623 hrs

22l Use Latin abbreviations sparingly

The following abbreviations, derived from Latin, are appropriate in academic writing. Be careful, however, not to overuse them.

Abbreviation	*Latin term*	*English meaning*
cf.	*confer*	compare
e.g.	*exempli gratia*	for example
et al.	*et alii*	and others
etc.	*et cetera*	and so forth
i.e.	*id est*	that is
N.B.	*nota bene*	note well

22m Use acronyms and initialisms only if their meaning is clear

WEBLINK

http://ccc.commnet.edu/
grammar/abbreviations.htm

A superb guide to
abbreviations

An initialism is an abbreviation formed from the first letters of a name—for example, *FBI* (for *Federal Bureau of Investigation*). Usually the letters are all capitalized. An **acronym** is an initialism that is pronounced as a word—for example, *ASCII, PAC, AIDS*. Some abbreviations, such as *JPEG, MS-DOS*, and *DRAM*, are *semi-acronyms:* part of the term is pronounced as one or more letters, the rest as a word (for example, "jay-peg"). As long as your audience knows what they mean and as long as you do not overdo it, there is nothing wrong with using such abbreviations where appropriate.

22n Avoid most other abbreviations in formal writing

Place names, including the names of states, countries, provinces, continents, and other localities, should not be abbreviated except in addresses and occasionally when used as adjectives (for example, in *US government*). Organization and company names should not be abbreviated unless they are extremely familiar (*UNESCO, IBM, UCLA*) or the full name has first been given. Fields of study should not be abbreviated. Write *political science* (not *poli sci*) and *psychology* (not *psych*).

NUMBERS

When you are writing text and need to cite a number, keep in mind the following guidelines.

 Use figures with abbreviations and conventionally numerical references

Time

7:00 a.m.	0700 hrs	seven o'clock in the morning
2:45 p.m.	1445 hrs	two forty-five in the afternoon

Dates

65 BC (or BCE)	AD 126 (or 126 CE)	the 1890s	May 15, 1996
from 1996 to 1998	1996–1998	1996–98	

Money

$23.4 billion $12,566 $7.99   45¢   forty-five cents   one dollar

Rates of speed

55 mph   33.6 bps   200 MHz
3000 rpm

WEBLINK

http://owl.english.purdue.edu/handouts/esl/eslnumber.html

An excellent guide to the use of numbers

Decimals and percentages

.05   5 percent (or 5%)

Telephone numbers

617-555-1284 [US]   +1 (617) 555 1284 [International]

Addresses

233 East 19th Street	PO Box 45	Route 66
New York, NY 10011		

Divisions of books and plays

volume 2, chapter 11, pages 346–55

King Lear, act II, scene i, lines 5–7 OR *King Lear* II.i.5–7

The Alchemist, act 2, scene 1, lines 5–7 OR *The Alchemist* 2.1.5–7

22p Write out other numbers that can be expressed in one or two words

One to ninety-nine

fifteen   twenty-two   eighty-four

Fractions

two-thirds   one-fourth   five-sixteenths

Large round numbers

thirteen hundred   four thousand   thirty million

Decades and centuries

the eighties (or the '80s)

the twenty-first century (or the 21st century)

22q Write out numbers that begin sentences

FAULTY   18% of Americans believe that career preparation should begin in elementary school.

REVISED   Eighteen percent of Americans believe that career preparation should begin in elementary school.

When a number is too large to write out (more than two words), keep the numerical form but rearrange the sentence so as to avoid beginning with a number.

FAULTY   240,183 people could be fed for one year with the food we Americans waste in one day.

REVISED   We Americans waste enough food in one day to feed 240,183 people for one year.

22r   Write one number as a figure and the other as a word when one number modifies another

We bought fourteen $25 tickets.

There were 75 twelfth-graders at the dance.

22s   Write related numbers in the same way

When comparing two or more numbers in the same sentence or paragraph, make the comparison easy to see by putting the numbers in the same form, as either words or figures.

It takes ~~nine hundred~~ hours of training to become a licensed hair braider in New York City but only 117 hours to become an emergency medical technician.

CHAPTER **23**

The Hyphen, Spelling, and Using a Thesaurus and Dictionary

THE HYPHEN

The hyphen (-) is typed as a single keystroke, with no space before or after. It differs from a dash, which is typed as two consecutive hyphens (--) and then usually converted by the computer into what looks like a long hyphen (—). The hyphen has two main functions: punctuating certain compound words and names (*self-destruct, fifty-fifty, Coca-Cola*) and dividing a word at the end of a line.

23a Consult your dictionary on hyphenating compounds

A **compound** is a word made up of two smaller words. Sometimes these smaller words are connected by a hyphen (*screen-test*), sometimes they are separated by a space (*screen pass*), and sometimes they are fused (*screensaver*). There are no firm rules for determining how to write a particular compound, so it is best to check your dictionary.

23b Hyphenate compounds acting as adjectives before nouns

When a compound is placed in front of a noun to act as a modifier, it is usually hyphenated.

I teach *seventh-grade* algebra.

Notice that the same compound, when *not* put before a noun, is *not* hyphenated.

> I teach algebra to the *seventh grade.*

Complex compounds are compounds made up of three or more words, like *cut-and-paste, ultra-high-density,* and *up-to-date.* When you hyphenate a complex compound, be sure to hyphenate all its parts— put hyphens between all the terms.

WEBLINK

http://www.grammarbook
.com/punctuation-hyphens
.html

All about hyphens

> I do a lot of *cut-and-paste* revising.

23c Hyphenate spelled-out fractions and numbers from twenty-one through ninety-nine

one-half   three-eighths   forty-four

23d Hyphenate to avoid ambiguity and awkward spellings

Some words, especially those with the prefix *re-, pre-,* or *anti-,* require hyphens to prevent misreadings, mispronunciations, and awkward-looking spellings:

> Now that Professor Muller has complicated the problem, we will
>
> *re-solve*
>
> have to ~~resolve~~ it.   [Without the hyphen, *re-solve,* "to solve again," would be read as *resolve,* "to deal with successfully."]

23e Use hyphens for end-of-line word division

In general, it is best to avoid dividing a word at the end of a line. But there are situations where word division is desirable. For example, if you are trying to arrange text in columns (in a brochure or résumé, for instance), end-of-line hyphentation may provide valuable extra space.

1. *Divide words only between syllables.* End-of-line hyphentation should occur only at syllable breaks.

2. *Avoid a second hyphen in a hyphenated word.* Words with prefixes like *self-*, *ex-*, and *all-* and complex compounds should not be hyphenated anywhere else.

   Jimmy Carter has set a new standard for civic activism by ex-~~Presi-~~
   Presidents
   ~~dents~~.

3. *Leave at least two letters on a line.* Do not divide a word so that a single letter is left hanging either on the first line or on the second line.

   emo-
   Stress management requires an examination of one's ~~e-~~
   tional
   ~~motional~~ responses to others.

4. *Avoid consecutive lines ending in hyphens.* Ending three or more lines in a row with hyphens draws attention and looks ungainly.

   Admitting to your feelings and allowing them to be expressed through either communication or action is a stress-
   management technique that can help you through many difficult situations.

SPELLING

Modern English is a product of many other languages, including German, French, Latin, Greek, Scandinavian, and Spanish. One unfortunate result of this hybridization is an irregular system of spelling that causes problems for many users of the language. If you are one of those people, be assured that you are not alone. However, it is important that you work on your spelling and keep trying to improve it. Many readers have little tolerance for bad spelling.

23f Use a spell checker

A computerized spell checker makes it easy to review for spelling errors. If you are not already doing so, you should routinely run a final spell check on any important document you write. Some word processors allow you to set the spell checker so that it will identify possible misspellings either while you are typing or after you have finished.

Spell checkers are far from perfect. Sometimes they flag words that are spelled correctly (especially names), and sometimes they fail to flag words that are spelled incorrectly.

Identifying misspellings that the spell checker missed is a more difficult problem. Spell checkers will accept any word that happens to match a word form in its dictionary, even if the word is misused. The most effective ways to avoid this problem are by (1) mastering troublesome homophones; (2) guarding against common spelling errors; and (3) learning some general spelling rules and patterns.

23g Master troublesome homophones

Homophones are words that sound alike but are spelled differently and have different meanings. They are one of the most common causes of misspelling in English and cannot be detected by a spell checker. For this reason, you should study them and learn their differences, especially those listed here:

its	possessive pronoun
it's	contraction of *it is*
loose	adjective: "free, not tightly secured"
lose	verb: "to fail to keep"
their	possessive form of *they*
there	adverb: "in that place"
they're	contraction of *they are*

to	preposition
too	adverb: "also"
two	adjective and noun: "2"
who's	contraction of *who is*
whose	possessive form of *who*
your	possessive form of *you*
you're	contraction of *you are*

23h Guard against common spelling errors

Although a spell checker can flag many spelling errors for you, it is still worth learning the correct spelling of the most commonly misspelled words. Some of these words follow.

Commonly Misspelled Words

accidentally	environment	necessary
accommodate	exaggerate	occurred
achieved	exceed	parallel
basically	February	receive
committee	government	separate
definitely	manageable	until
dependent		

23i Learn general spelling rules and patterns

Although English is not the simplest language in the world to learn when it comes to spelling, it does have a number of general rules and patterns that make things easier.

1 Prefixes

Prefixes are small word parts, like *re-*, *anti-*, and *pre-*, placed at the beginnings of words. Prefixes do not change the spelling of the root word: *anti-* added to *-freeze* becomes *antifreeze*. In some cases, though, a hyphen is required: *anti-* plus *-intellectual* is spelled *anti-intellectual*.

mis + spell = misspell
un + necessary = unnecessary

2 Suffixes

Suffixes are small word parts, like *-age*, *-ence*, *-ing*, and *-tion*, placed at the ends of words. By adding suffixes to a root word such as *sense-*, you can create different meanings: *sensitive, sensual, sensory, senseless*. In doing so, however, you must observe the following spelling rules.

   1. If the word ends in a silent *e* and the suffix starts with a vowel, drop the *e*.

   imagine + ation = imagination

There are some exceptions. Some words need to retain the *e* in order to be distinguished from similar words (*dyeing/dying*), to prevent mispronunciation (*mileage, being*), or to keep a soft *c* or *g* sound (*noticeable, courageous*).

   2. If the word ends in a silent *e* and the suffix starts with a consonant, do not drop the *e*.

   require + ment = requirement

   spine + less = spineless

Some exceptions are *argument, awful, ninth, truly*, and *wholly*.

   3. When adding a suffix to a word that ends in *y*, change the *y* to *i* if the letter preceding the *y* is a consonant.

   study + ous = studious

   comply + ance = compliance

Exceptions are words with the suffix *-ing*, which keep the *y* in all cases: *studying, carrying, drying, paying*.

   4. In creating adverbs from adjectives, add *-ly* to the adjective unless the adjective ends in *-ic*, in which case use *-ally*.

   silent + ly = silently

   vile + ly = vilely

5. In choosing between *-able* and *-ible*, use *-able* if the root word can stand alone; otherwise, use *-ible*.

understand + able = understandable

change + able = changeable

vis + ible = visible

6. Double the final consonant of the root word if (a) the root word ends with a single accented vowel and a single consonant and (b) the suffix begins with a vowel.

drop + ed = dropped

slim + er = slimmer

3 Plurals

English has several different ways of forming plurals from singular nouns. Following are some rules for forming plurals.

1. For most words, add *s*.

tool, tools   minute, minutes

2. For words ending with *s, sh, ch, x,* or *z*, add *es*.

bus, buses   sandwich, sandwiches
quiz, quizzes   [Note the doubled final consonant.]

3. For words ending with a consonant followed by *y*, change the *y* to *i* and add *es*.

enemy, enemies   strawberry, strawberries

4. For some words ending with *f* or *fe*, change the *f* or *fe* to *v* and add *es*.

half, halves   thief, thieves

Some exceptions are *belief, beliefs; chief, chiefs; proof, proofs;* and *motif, motifs.*

5. For compound nouns written as single words, add the plural ending as you would to an ordinary noun.

laptop, laptops   database, databases

6. For compound nouns written as two or more words or hyphenated, add the plural ending to the noun being modified.

video game, video games   [The noun being modified is *game*.]
word processor, word processors   [The noun being modified is *processor*.]

Irregular plurals must be learned individually. Sometimes, an internal vowel must be changed to make a noun plural:

woman, women   mouse, mice

With some nouns derived from Latin or Greek, a final *us, um,* or *on* must be changed to *i* or *a*:

syllabus, syllabi   medium, media   criterion, criteria

Some nouns have the same form for both singular and plural:

deer, deer   species, species

4 The "*i* before *e*" rule

The rule you had to memorize in elementary school is worth keeping in mind: "*i* before *e* except after *c* or when sounded like *ay*, as in *neighbor* or *weigh*."

I BEFORE *E*

achieve   field

EXCEPT AFTER *C*

ceiling   receive

OR WHEN SOUNDED LIKE *AY*

eight   vein

Some exceptions are *ancient, caffeine, conscience, counterfeit, either, foreign, height, leisure, neither, seize, science,* and *weird*.

USING A THESAURUS AND DICTIONARY

A writer needs tools, and two of the best are a good thesaurus and a good dictionary.

23j   Use a thesaurus to find the exact word

Part of being a good writer is choosing words that accurately express your thoughts. A thesaurus is a listing of synonyms and antonyms that allows you to zero in on the exact word you are looking for.

1 Electronic thesaurus

Today, most word-processing programs have a built-in thesaurus, which you can use as you write. (It is usually on the same menu as the spell checker.) You can also find thesauruses on the Internet. Or, you can buy a thesaurus on a CD-ROM, either by itself or as a supplement to a dictionary.

2 Traditional thesaurus

You should also feel comfortable using a thesaurus in traditional book form. The pocket-size versions are handy for carrying around; larger, desk-size thesauruses are found in all libraries and many offices. In many pocket-size thesauruses, the words are arranged alphabetically, as in a dictionary.

23k   Use a dictionary to learn about words

Traditional, printed dictionaries come in two types: pocket size and desk size. The pocket size is handy, but the desk size contains more complete information. Electronic dictionaries usually have as much information as desk-size types and can be found in CD-ROM format or on the Internet.

1 Spelling, word division, and pronunciation

A typical dictionary entry begins with the main word, correctly spelled and divided into syllables: *ha-rass*. Knowing where to divide a word is helpful for typing if you do not use automatic hyphenation on your computer. If a word has two correct spellings, they are both listed, with the preferred spelling first. The word's pronunciation is indicated next, in parentheses: (hăr´əs, hə-răs´), with the preferred form first. Most modern dictionaries have a pronunciation key at the bottom of the page to help you decipher the pronunciation. For words of more than one syllable, a heavy accent mark (´) indicates which syllable should receive primary stress; some words have a secondary accent (´) as well. Some electronic dictionaries allow you to click on a button and get a voice recording of the correct pronunciation of the word.

WEBLINK

http://writing.colostate.edu/links/index.cfm?category=writers

Direct access to the best online dictionaries and thesauruses

2 Parts of speech, word endings, and word senses

Next come symbols describing some aspect of the word—for example, what part of speech it is (such as a noun, verb, or adjective) or whether it is singular or plural. The most common abbreviations are these:

adj.	adjective	*intr.*	intransitive	*pron.*	pronoun
adv.	adverb	*n.*	noun	*sing.*	singular
aux.	auxiliary	*pl.*	plural	*suff.*	suffix
conj.	conjunction	*pref.*	prefix	*tr.*	transitive
interj.	interjection	*prep.*	preposition	*v.*	verb

Often an entry will include variants of the main word, showing different word endings.

Many words have more than one meaning, or sense. Each sense has a separate listing, generally preceded by a boldface number. In some dictionaries, these senses are arranged historically, according to when they entered the language; in other dictionaries, senses are listed according to current popularity, with the most commonly used sense appearing first.

3 Etymology, related words, synonyms, and usage

Information about a word's origin, or etymology, is given in square brackets. This information can help you to learn the word and use it accurately.

Sometimes, related words—words derived from the same root—are given as well.

Some dictionaries list **synonyms** for certain words, along with explanations of the differences among them and examples. Also, some dictionaries provide usage notes, which typically represent the judgments of a panel of authorities about "correct" usage. In many dictionaries, particular senses of a word may be given usage labels such as *Informal, Colloquial, Non-Standard, Slang, Vulgar, Obscene, Offensive, Archaic,* or *Obsolete.* You may want to check the front of your dictionary to see how the different kinds of usage are defined.

CHAPTER 24

Tips on Nouns, Articles, Verbs, Word Order, and Vocabulary

NOUNS AND ARTICLES

Articles (*a, an, the*) are important in the English language because they clarify what nouns refer to. There is a significant difference in meaning between "I found *a* new Web site" and "I found *the* new Web site." The first sentence introduces new information, while the second sentence implies that the new Web site is something the reader or listener already knew about. Articles can be used to mark other subtleties as well. Because many other languages do not use articles in this way, though, many nonnative speakers of English have trouble with articles.

24a Use the plural only with count nouns

To use articles correctly, you first need a clear understanding of the difference between count nouns and noncount nouns. Count nouns refer to things that have a distinct physical or mental form and thus can be counted, like *book, apple, diskette, scientist*, and *idea*. Count nouns can be enumerated and pluralized—for example, *eight books, three apples, several diskettes, two scientists*, and *many ideas*.

WEBLINK

http://leo.stcloudstate.edu/
grammar/countnon.html

Help with count and
noncount nouns

Noncount (or mass) nouns are words like *air, rice, electricity, excitement,* and *coverage* that do not have a distinct form as a whole. (Though each grain of rice may have a distinct form, rice as a mass quantity is variable in form.) Noncount nouns are neither enumerated nor pluralized. No one would say *eight airs, three rices, several electricities, two excitements,* or *many coverages.*

Noncount nouns are quantified with expressions like *a lot of, much, some,* and *a cup of*—for example, *some air, a cup of rice, much excitement,* and *a lot of coverage.*

24b Use *the* for specific references

In deciding whether to use *the, a, an,* or no article at all, keep in mind the concept of specificity. Does the noun refer to some particular thing or set of things, or does it refer to something general? As mentioned in the introduction to this chapter, "*the* Web site" refers to specific, unique Web site, whereas "*a* Web site" refers to any Web site.

1 Using *the* with superlative adjectives
Adjectives like *best, worst,* and *most interesting* single out one particular thing among many.

2 Using *the* with unique things
The past, the present, the sun, and *the solar system* all have unique identities. There is only one past, only one present, only one sun (in our solar system anyway).

> Thirty minutes after boarding, the plane was still on *the ground.*

3 Using *the* with nouns followed by a modifier
Many nouns are followed by a phrase or clause that restricts the noun's identity.

> *The theory <u>of relatively</u>* was developed by Einstein.
>
> *The girl <u>in the corner</u>* is in my physics class.

4 Using *the* to refer to something previously mentioned

Once something has been mentioned, it becomes part of the reader's knowledge. When you refer to it again, use *the* so that the reader knows that you are talking about the same thing.

> I went shopping today and bought some beans, rice, and *chicken*.

> We can cook *the chicken* for dinner.

Note: For clarity or emphasis, the demonstrative adjective *this, that, those,* or *these* may sometimes be used instead of *the*.

5 Using *the* to draw on shared knowledge

If you and your reader can draw on shared experience to identify something in particular, use *the* to mark it.

> Please shut down *the computer* when you are done with it.

6 Using *the* for contextual specificity

Sometimes the context of a situation allows you and your reader to identify something as unique. Consider, for example, the word *printer*. There are many printers in the world, but if you are writing about a computer and you want to mention the printer attached to it, use *the* to indicate that it is the only printer in this particular context.

> I was using my friend's computer and could not get *the printer* to work.

7 Using *the* to denote an entire class of things

The can be used with a singular count noun to denote an entire class or genre of things.

> *The earthworm* is one of nature's most valuable creatures.

24c Use *the* with most proper nouns derived from common nouns

Proper nouns are names of things such as persons, places, holidays, religions, companies, and organizations. Most proper nouns, even though they uniquely identify somebody or something, do not take the definite article:

Muhammad Ali   Mother Theresa   New York   Microsoft

Many proper nouns, though, do take the definite article:

the Rolling Stones   the United States
the Panama Canal   the International Red Cross

Those that take the definite article have a head noun derived from a common English noun: *stones, states, canal, cross.*

There are many exceptions, however, to this pattern: *Elm Street, Salt Lake City, Carleton College, Princeton University, Lookout Mountain.* We suggest that you pay close attention to each proper name you encounter and note whether it is used with *the.*

24d Use *a* or *an* in nonspecific references to singular count nouns

Nonspecific nouns refer to *types* of things rather than to specific things. With nonspecific singular count nouns, such as *shirt, jacket, belt,* and *hat,* you must use an indefinite article (either *a* or, if the next sound is a vowel sound, *an*) or some other determiner (for example, *my, your, this,* or *each*).

I bought *a shirt* and *an overcoat.*

24e Use no article in nonspecific references to plural count nouns or noncount nouns

With nonspecific plural count nouns, such as *shirts, jackets, belts,* and *hats,* no article is used. You may use, however, determiners like *our, some, these,* and *no.*

There were *socks* and *shorts* on sale, but *no belts.*

PHRASAL VERBS

Phrasal verbs are made up of a verb and one or two **particles** (prepositions or adverbs)—for example, *pick over, look into, get away with.* They are sometimes called two-word verbs or three-word verbs. Phrasal verbs are common in English, especially in informal speech. Some phrasal verbs mean something quite different from their associated simple verbs. For example, if a friend of yours says, "I just *ran into* Nguyen in the library," the encounter probably had nothing to do with running. *To run into* means "to encounter unintentionally." Other phrasal verbs are used merely to intensify the meaning of the simple verb. For example, *fill up* is a more emphatic version of *fill*.

Some phrasal verbs are **transitive** (that is, they have direct objects), while others are **intransitive**. For example, *dig up* (meaning "find") is transitive ("I *dug up* some information for my paper"), but *speak up* (meaning "speak louder") is intransitive ("Please *speak up*"). Some phrasal verbs have both transitive and intransitive meanings. For example, *show up* can mean either "expose or embarrass (someone)" or "arrive," depending on whether it is used transitively or intransitively. "He tried to *show up* the teacher" (transitive) versus "He never *shows up* on time" (intransitive).

Some transitive phrasal verbs are **separable,** meaning that the particle may be placed after the object of the verb: "I quickly *looked over* my paper" or "I quickly *looked* my paper *over*." Other transitive phrasal verbs are **inseparable,** meaning that the verb and the particle must be kept together: "I quickly *went over* my paper," not "I quickly *went* my paper *over*."

VERB COMPLEMENTS

Verb complements include gerunds (*swimming*), *to* infinitives (*to swim*), and un-marked infinitives (*swim*). English verbs differ in the kinds of verb complements they can take.

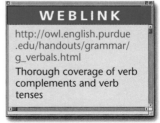

WEBLINK

http://owl.english.purdue.edu/handouts/grammar/g_verbals.html

Thorough coverage of verb complements and verb tenses

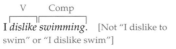

V — Comp

I *dislike swimming*. [Not "I dislike to swim" or "I dislike swim"]

V — Comp

I *want to swim*. [Not "I want swimming" or "I want swim"]

$$\overset{\text{V}}{\overbrace{}}\ \overset{\text{Comp}}{\overbrace{}}$$
I *like swimming*. OR I *like to swim*.   [Not "I like swim"]

$$\overset{\text{V}}{\overbrace{}}\ \overset{\text{Comp}}{\overbrace{}}$$
I *made* her *swim*.   [Not "I made her swimming" or "I made her to swim"]

24f Learn which verbs take gerunds as complements

The following verbs take gerunds (verbals ending in *ing*), but not infinitives, as complements, as in "Maria *acknowledged skipping* class."

acknowledge	cannot (can't) help	detest	evade
admit	consider	discuss	finish
advise	consist of	dislike	give up
anticipate	delay	dream about	have trouble
appreciate	deny	enjoy	imagine
avoid	depend on	escape	insist on

24g Learn which verbs take *to* infinitives as complements

The following verbs take *to* infinitives, but not participles, as complements, as in "Kim cannot *afford to buy* a car."

afford	decide	intend	offer	seem
agree	demand	learn	plan	struggle
ask	expect	like	prepare	tend
attempt	fail	manage	pretend	threaten
claim	hesitate	mean	promise	wait
consent	hope	need	refuse	want

24h Learn which verbs take either gerunds or *to* infinitives as complements

The following verbs can take either a gerund or a *to* infinitive as a complement: "He *began learning* English as a small child" or "He *began to learn* English as a small child."

begin	dread	like	stop*
cannot (can't) stand	forget*	love	try
continue	hate	remember*	

For those verbs marked with an asterisk, the meaning of the sentence depends on the type of complement: "He *forgot to go* to the store" means that he did not go to the store, while "He *forgot going* to the store" means that he did go to the store but then did not remember going there.

24i Learn which verbs take only unmarked infinitives as complements

Some verbs, when followed by a noun or pronoun, take an infinitive without *to* (an "unmarked" infinitive), as in "She *let him pay* for dinner." Such verbs include

have   help   let   make

(Note that *help* can also take a *to* infinitive as a complement.)

VERBS OF STATE

Many English verbs depict states or conditions rather than events or actions. These verbs are called **verbs of state**.

24j Do not use the progressive aspect with verbs of state

Verbs of state generally do not take on the progressive aspect. For example, *consist of* is a verb of state and therefore cannot occur in the progressive.

> *consists*
> The program ~~is consisting~~ of four parts.

The following verbs do not take on the progressive aspect:

appear	constitute	exist	need	seem
believe	contain	involve	possess	suppose
belong	correspond	know	represent	understand
consist of	differ from	mean	result in	want

MODAL AUXILIARY VERBS

The **modal auxiliary verbs** include *can, could, may, might, must, will, would,* and *should.* They are used to express a variety of conditions including possibility, necessity, ability, permission, and obligation. Each modal auxiliary has at least two principal meanings, one relating to social interaction and the other to logical probability. For example, the word *may* in a sentence like. "*May* I sit down?" requests permission, an aspect of social interaction, while the word *may* in a sentence like "It *may* rain today" denotes logical possibility. Within these two general categories, the modal auxiliaries carry different degrees of strength. Modal auxiliary verbs have certain distinct grammatical features that can cause problems for nonnative speakers.

 24k Use only a base verb form immediately after a modal auxiliary

Any verb immediately following a modal auxiliary must be in the base, or simple, form (for example, *teach, have, go, run*), not in the *to* infinitive or gerund form.

NO   History *can to teach* us many good lessons.

YES   History *can teach* us many good lessons.

24l Do not use more than one modal at a time

NO   If I study hard, I *might could* get an A.

YES   If I study hard, I *might* get an A.

YES   If I study hard, I *could* get an A.

If you want to combine a modal auxiliary verb with some other modal meaning, use a modal phrase such as *be able to*, *be allowed to*, or *have to*.

YES   If I study hard, I *might be able to* get an A.

CONDITIONAL SENTENCES

Conditional sentences have two parts: a subordinate clause beginning with *if* (or *when* or *unless*) that sets a condition and a main clause that expresses a result. The tense and mood of the verb in the subordinate clause depend on the tense and mood of the verb in the main clause. There are three main types of conditional sentences: factual, predictive, and hypothetical.

 24m In factual conditionals, use the same verb tense in both parts

Factual conditional sentences depict factual relationships. The conditional clause begins with *if, when, whenever,* or some other condition-setting expression; the conditional clause verb is cast in the same tense as the result clause verb.

If you don't *get* enough rest, you *get* tired.

24n In predictive conditionals, use a present-tense verb in the *if* clause and an appropriate modal in the result clause

Predictive conditional sentences express future possible conditions and results. The conditional clause starts with *if* or *unless* and has a present-tense verb; the result clause verb is formed with a modal (*will, can, should, may,* or *might*) and the base form of the verb.

If we *leave* now, we *can be* there by 5 o'clock.

24o In hypothetical conditionals, use a past-tense verb in the *if* clause and *would, could,* or *might* in the result clause

Hypothetical conditional sentences depict situations that are unlikely to happen or are contrary to fact. For hypothetical past situations, the verb in the conditional clause should be in the past perfect tense and the verb in the main clause should be formed from *would have, could have,* or *might have* and the past participle.

> If we *had invested* our money in stocks instead of bonds, we *would have gained* a lot more.

For hypothetical present or future situations, the verb in the conditional clause should be in the past tense and the verb in the main clause should be formed from *would, could,* or *might* and the base form.

> If we *invested* our money in stocks instead of bonds, we *would gain* a lot more.

TIPS ON WORD ORDER

Unlike many other languages, English depends on word order to convey meaning. A change in word order often produces a different meaning. For example, "Kevin likes Maria" means something quite different from "Maria likes Kevin." This section discusses word-order patterns involving strings of adjectives, compound nouns, and adverb placement.

24p String adjectives in the order preferred in English

If you string two or more adjectives together, you have to put them in the appropriate order.

FAULTY   The *wood broken* fence will be repaired.

REVISED   The *broken wood* fence will be repaired.

The following list shows the preferred ordering of adjectives in English:

1. Article or determiner: *the, a, an, my, our, Carla's, this, that, those*
2. Ordinal expression: *first, second, last, next, final*
3. Quantity: *one, two, few, many, some*
4. Evaluation: *beautiful, delicious, interesting, unfortunate, ugly*
5. Size: *tiny, small, short, tall, large, big*
6. Shape: *square, oval, cylindrical, round*
7. Condition: *shiny, clean, dirty, broken*
8. Age: *new, young, old, ancient*
9. Color: *black, red, yellow, green, white*
10. Nationality: *Mexican, Chinese, Vietnamese, Japanese*
11. Religion: *Catholic, Confucian, Buddhist, Muslim*
12. Material: *cotton, stone, plastic, gold*
13. Special use or purpose (may be a noun used as an adjective): *carving, carrying, sports, medical, computer*
14. The noun being modified

Here are some expressions created by following the preferred ordering:

1	2	3	4	5	6	7	8	9	10	11	12	13	14
The	first			small	/	shiny	new		Japanese			sports	car
A		few					young			Buddhist			monks
Her		favorite		long				yellow			silk		flowers

24q String nouns for easiest recognition

Stringing nouns together to form noun compounds is common in English. Terms like *bike lock, keyboard, houseboat, picnic table,* and *bookmark* were formed by putting two ordinary nouns together. And it is easy to add a third noun to make them more descriptive: *combination bike lock, keyboard cover, houseboat community, picnic table leg,* and *bookmark program.*

In all noun compounds, the rightmost noun is the head noun and the nouns preceding it serve as modifiers. These modifier nouns can modify either the head noun or another modifier noun.

Modifier	Head		Modifier	Head
Noun	Noun		Noun	Noun

combination bike lock   mountain bike lock

Nouns used as modifiers typically lose any plural endings they might have. Someone who loves movies is a *movie lover*, not a *movies lover*; the juice from cranberries is *cranberry juice*, not *cranberries juice*.

24r Use meaning to place adverbs that modify verbs

Adverbs can modify verbs, adjectives, other adverbs, or entire sentences. Adverbs that modify verbs can be placed at either the beginning, the middle, or the end of a clause, depending on their meaning.

1 Placing adverbs of frequency

Adverbs of frequency (*usually, seldom, always, never*) are usually placed directly before the main verb (and after the auxiliary verb, if there is one).

> Tim says he *usually* writes his papers on time, yet he is *always* turning them in late.

Some adverbs of frequency (*often, twice, many times*) can also be placed at the end of the clause.

> He has missed class *quite often*.

2 Placing adverbs of time when

Adverbs of time when (*yesterday, at eight o'clock, last year*) are normally placed at the end of the clause.

> The exhibit will open *next month*.

3 Placing adverbs of place

Adverbs of place (*upstairs, in the park, under a tree*) usually follow the verb. However, they should not intervene between the verb and an object.

> She took her dog for a walk *in the park*.

24s Place adverbs directly before adjectives or adverbs that they modify

An adverb that modifies an adjective or another adverb should be placed directly before the word it modifies.

Jose is an *unusually quick* learner. He concentrates *very intensely* on his studies.

24t Place adverbs before sentences or clauses that they modify

An adverb that modifies a whole sentence or clause is usually placed at the beginning of the sentence or clause.

Unfortunately, his younger brother Ramon does not follow his example.

24u Do not put an adverb between a verb and its object

Nonnative speakers sometimes make the mistake of positioning an adverb between the verb and its object or objects.

FAULTY   Javier writes *often* letters to his family.

REVISED   Javier *often* writes letters to his family.

TIPS ON VOCABULARY

Many nonnative speakers of English feel that they just do not know enough words to express their thoughts as fully as they would like. This section covers some of the most common vocabulary problems for nonnative speakers—those related to cognates, collocations, and idioms.

24v Look for cognates, but watch out for "false friends"

Cognates are words that have a formal relation to similar words in another language. They are usually quite recognizable. For example, the English *telephone* and Spanish *teléfono* are cognates, and it is easy for speakers of either language to recognize this word when learning the other language.

If your native language is closely related to English, cognate recognition is a good strategy for learning new words. In most cases, you can trust a cognate to carry more or less the same meaning in your second language as it has in your first language. Of course, there are often subtle differences that you should pay attention to. For example, although the word *collar* is used in both English and Spanish to refer to the band around the neck of an animal, in Spanish it is also used to mean "necklace."

Sometimes, however, words that look similar in two different languages have entirely different meanings. These words are called **false cognates** or false friends. An example of a false cognate is the English *jubilation* and Spanish *jubilación*. The English word means "happiness," while the Spanish one means "retirement, pension (money)." You should always be on the alert for false cognates. Never assume that two words mean the same thing just because they look similar.

24w Try to get a feel for collocations

Collocations are words that commonly occur together. For example, the word *advice* commonly occurs with the verbs *give, get,* and *receive* and with the adjectives *good, bad,* and *sound.* This is why the sentence "She gave me some good advice" sounds like normal American English, while the sentence "She presented me some nice advice" does not.

rise
A steep ~~upshoot~~ in grain prices could topple many governments in the Third World.

broad
Lazy thinkers tend to make ~~wide~~ generalizations about things.

The best way to develop your knowledge of collocations is to pay attention to them in the English you see and hear around you. In this way, you will develop a feel for which words go with which.

24x Learn idioms in their entirety

A special type of collocation, an **idiomatic expression,** or idiom, is a fixed phrase whose meaning cannot be deduced from the meanings of its parts. For example, even if you know the words *kick* and *bucket,* you may not know what the idiom *kick the bucket* means (it means "die"). The same holds true for other idioms like *beat around the bush, have a screw loose,* or *lip service.* Because of their unpredictability, you have to learn idioms in their entirety, one at a time. And you have to use them in exactly the right form. If you said *kick a bucket* or *kick the pail,* many listeners would not understand what you meant. Many idioms involve phrasal verbs.

The best way to learn a language's idioms is by listening to native speakers. Some good Web sites can also be of help: Dave Sperling's Idiom Page at *http://www.pacificnet.net/~sperling/idioms.cgi,* The Weekly Idiom at *http://simsim .rug.ac.be/staff/elke/ltolpres8mei/idiom.html,* and Vocabulary on the Internet at *http://ec.hku.hk/vec/vocab/vocint.htm.*

Glossary of Grammatical and Rhetorical Terms

absolute phrase A subject and an adjective phrase (often a participial phrase) used to modify an entire clause. (9c-2)

abstract noun A word that names an idea, emotion, quality, or other intangible concept—for example, *beauty, passion, despair*. (9a-1, 17a-2)

acronym A pronounceable word that is formed from the first letters of a multi-word name and is usually written in uppercase letters. (22m)

active voice The form a transitive verb takes to indicate that the subject is performing the action on the direct object. (9a-3, 10q)

adjective A word that modifies a noun by qualifying or describing it. (9a-5, Chapter 10)

adjective clause A dependent clause, usually introduced by a relative pronoun, that modifies a noun or pronoun. (9c-3)

adverb A word that modifies a verb, adjective, clause, sentence, or other adverb. (9a-6, Chapter 10, 24r, 24u)

adverb clause A dependent clause that begins with a subordinating conjunction and answers the question when, where, how, or why. (9c-3).

agreement The grammatical requirement that a verb and its subject have the same number (either plural or singular), and that a pronoun and its antecedent have the same number and gender. (Chapter 12)

antecedent The noun that precedes and is replaced by a pronoun. A pronoun should agree in number and gender with its antecedent. (9a-2, 10a, 10b)

appositive A special type of pronoun-noun pairing in which a pronoun is conjoined with a noun. (10g)

appositive phrase A noun phrase, placed next to another noun, that describes or defines the other noun and is usually set off by commas. (9c-2, 15i)

article A word that precedes a noun and indicates definiteness or indefiniteness. Standard Edited English has three articles: *a, an, the*. (9a-1, 24a–d)

attributive possessive pronoun A possessive pronoun used directly before a noun. (10i)

auxiliary verb   A verb, such as *has*, *be*, or *do*, that combines with a main verb to form a simple predicate. (9a-3)

case   The form a pronoun takes to indicate its grammatical relation to other words in the sentence. (10e) See also objective case, subjective case.

clause   A group of words that has a subject and a predicate. Compare with *phrase*. (9c-3)

clustering   A prewriting technique that helps a writer to see relationships among ideas. (1b-4)

cognates   Two words, from different languages, that are similar in form and meaning. (24v)

collective noun   A singular word that names a group. (9a-1)

collocations   Two or more words that frequently occur together. (24w)

comma splice   Two independent clauses joined only by a comma. (Chapter 11)

common noun   A word that names one or more persons, places, things, or qualities as a general category. (9a-1)

complete predicate   The simple predicate plus any objects, complements, or adverbial modifiers. (9b-2, 9b-3)

complex compound   A word made up of three or more words. (23b)

complex sentence   A sentence that has a single independent clause and one or more dependent clauses. (9d-2, 21o)

complex series   A series in which individual items contain internal commas, necessitating the use of semicolons to separate the items. (19m)

compound   A word made up of two smaller words. (23a)

compound antecedent   A noun phrase consisting of two or more terms joined by *and*. (10a)

compound-complex sentence   A sentence that has two or more independent clauses and one or more dependent clauses. (9d-2, 15o)

compound predicate   A predicate containing two or more verbs with the same subject. (9b-2)

compound sentence   A sentence that has two or more independent clauses and no dependent clauses. (9d-2, 21o)

compound subject   A sentence subject consisting of two or more simple subjects. (9b-2)

concrete noun   A word that names something that can be touched, seen, heard, smelled, or tasted. (9a-2, 17a-2)

conjunction   A word that joins two sentences, clauses, phrases, or words. (9a-8)

conjunctive adverb   An adverb that modifies an entire sentence or clause while linking it to the preceding sentence or clause. (9a-6, 15h, 19f)

connotation   Extra nuances or meaning that a word has, beyond its basic meaning. (17b)

contraction   A reduced form of a word or pair of words. (17c-2)

coordinate adjectives   A series of adjectives, separated by commas, that could be arranged in any order. (19d)

coordinating conjunction   A conjunction used to connect sentences, clauses, phrases, or words that are parallel in meaning. (21h, 9a-8, 15g)

coordination   The pairing of equivalent sentences or sentence elements by putting them in the same grammatical form and linking them via a coordinating conjunction, conjunctive adverb, or semicolon. (15h)

correlative conjunctions   Conjunctions that are used in pairs. (9a-8, 15k)

count noun   A word that names something that can be counted and pluralized. (9a, 24a)

cumulative adjectives   A series of adjectives, each one modifying those following it. (24a)

dangling modifier   An introductory verbal phrase that does not refer to the subject of the sentence. (13e)

demonstrative adjective   An adjective that singles out a specific noun. (9a-5, 10s)

demonstrative pronoun   A pronoun that points to its antecedent noun. (9a-2)

denotation   The basic dictionary meaning of a word. (17a)

dependent clause   A clause that cannot stand alone as a sentence but must be attached to a main clause. (9c-2, 11b)

diction   A writer's choice of words (Chapter 17)

direct discourse   Language that is taken word for word from another source and is enclosed in quotation marks. (14f)

direct object   A noun, pronoun, or noun phrase that completes the action of the verb in an active sentence. (9b-2)

disjunctive antecedent   A noun phrase consisting of two or more terms joined by *or* or *nor*. (10a)

disjunctive subject   A sentence subject consisting of two nouns or pronouns joined by *or* or *nor*. (12c)

double negative   Sentence or phrase containing two negative modifiers that carry the same meaning. (10x)

false cognates   Two words, from different languages, that resemble each other but have different meanings. (24v)

future perfect progressive tense   A verb tense formed by combining *will have been* and the –*ing* form of the main verb. (10n-3)

future perfect tense   A verb tense formed by combining *will have* and the past participle of the main verb. (10n-3)

future progressive tense   A verb tense formed by combining *will be* and the –*ing* form of the main verb. (10n-3)

future tense   A verb tense formed by combining the modal auxiliary *will* and the base form of the main verb. (10n-3)

generic pronoun   A pronoun used to refer to all people regardless of gender. (17g-2)

gerund   A verb form that ends in –*ing* and functions as a noun. (9c-2)

gerund phrase   A phrase consisting of a gerund and any modifiers, objects, and/or complements. (9c-2)

idiomatic expression   A phrase whose meaning cannot be deduced from the meanings of its individual words. (17c-2, 21i)

imperative mood   A grammatical form of a verb used to express a command or give instructions. (9a-3, 10r, 14b)

imperative sentence   A sentence that expresses a command or request, usually with an understood subject *you*. (9d-1)

independent clause   A group of words that includes a subject and predicate and can stand alone as a sentence. (9c-3)

indicative mood   A grammatical form of a verb used to make assertions, state opinions, and ask questions. (9a-3, 10r)

indirect discourse   A summarization, restatement, or paraphrase of a statement made by someone else. (14f, 20d)

indirect object   A noun, pronoun, or noun phrase that is indirectly affected by the action of the verb. (9b-2)

infinitive   The base form of a verb usually preceded by *to*. (9a-4, 10o-3)

infinitive phrase   A phrase consisting of an infinitive and any modifiers, objects, and/or complements. (9c-2)

inseparable verb   A transitive phrasal verb whose particle must be kept together with the verb. (Chapter 24)

intensive pronoun   A pronoun that consists of a personal pronoun plus –*self* or –*selves* and is used for emphasis. (9a-2)

interrogative adjective   An adjective that raises a question about a noun. (9a-5, 10s)

interrogative pronoun   A pronoun that introduces a question. (9a-2, 10h)

interrogative sentence   A sentence that raises a question and is punctuated with a question mark. (9d-1)

intransitive verb   A verb that does not take a direct object. (9a-3, 10f, Chapter 24)

irregular verb   A verb whose past tense and past participle are not formed through the standard pattern of adding *d* or *ed* to the base form. (10b)

linking verb   A verb that joins a sentence subject to a subject complement, indicating a condition, quality, or state of being. (9b-3)

metaphor   A figure of speech in which the writer describes something in a way normally reserved for something else, thus presenting it in a new light. (23f)

mixed construction   An ungrammatical sentence that starts one way but finishes in another. (20f)

modal auxiliary verb   A special type of verb that indicates necessity, probability, or permission. (19a-3, 10m, 24k)

modifier   A word, phrase, or clause that adds detail to another word, phrase, or clause. (9c, Chapter 19)

mood   The form of a verb that indicates the type of statement made—indicative, imperative, or subjunctive. (9a-3, 10h, 14b)

noncount noun   A word that names something that typically is not counted or pluralized, also called a *mass noun*. (9a, 24a)

nonrestrictive element   A phrase or clause that provides extra information in a sentence. (19e)

noun   A word that names a person, place, thing, quality, idea, or action. (9a-1)

noun clause   A dependent clause that begins with a relative pronoun and functions as a sentence subject, object, complement, or appositive. (9c-3)

object complement   A noun, noun phrase, adjective, or adjective phrase that elaborates or describes the direct object of a sentence. (9b-2)

object of the preposition   A noun or pronoun in a prepositional phrase. (9a-7)

objective case   The form a pronoun takes when it is used as a grammatical object. (10f)

parallelism   The use of similar grammatical form for words or phrases that have a coordinate relationship. (Chapter 15)

participial phrase   A phrase consisting of a present or past participle plus any objects, modifiers, and/or complements. (9c-2)

participle   A verb form that can serve as an adjective. (9a-4)

particle   A preposition or adverb that, when attached to a verb, creates a phrasal verb. (9a-7)

passive voice   The form a transitive verb takes to indicate that the subject is being acted on. (9a-3, 10g)

past participle   A verb form that can be used by itself as an adjective or can be combined with some form of the auxiliary *have* to form perfect tenses or with some form of the verb *be* to create passive-voice sentences. (10k, 10o-4)

past perfect progressive tense   A verb tense formed by combining *had been* and the present participle of the main verb. (10n-2)

past perfect tense   A verb tense created by combining *had* and the past participle of the main verb. (10n-2)

past progressive tense   A verb tense formed by combining the auxiliary verb *was* or *were* and the present participle of the main verb. (10n-2)

past tense   A verb tense that indicates past action. (10k, 10n-2)

perfect infinitive   A verb form consisting of *to have* plus the past participle of the verb. (10n-3)

personal pronoun   A pronoun that refers to one or more specific persons, places, or things. (9a-2)

phrasal verb   A verb consisting of a verb and one or two particles. (9a-7, Chapter 24)

phrase   A group of related words that does not have both a subject and a complete predicate. (9c-2)

plagiarism   Unauthorized or misleading use of the language and thoughts of another author. (3c-3)

predicate   The part of a sentence that contains the verb and makes a statement about the subject. (9b-2)

predicate adjective   An adjective that follows a linking verb and refers back to the noun subject. (9a-5)

prefix   A word part, such as *anti-*, *re-*, or *dis-*, that is attached to the beginning of a word. (23i-1)

preposition   A word that indicates a relationship between a noun or pronoun and some other parts of the sentence. (9a-7)

prepositional phrase   A group of words consisting of a preposition plus a noun or pronoun and its modifiers. (9a-7, 9c-2)

present infinitive   A verb form consisting of *to* plus the base form of the verb. (10o-3)

present participle   A verb form created by adding *–ing* to the base form. (10k, 10o-3)

present perfect participle   A verb form consisting of *having* plus the past participle of the verb. (10o-4).

present perfect progressive tense   A verb tense formed by combining *have been* or *has been* and the present participle of the main verb. (10n-1)

present perfect tense   A verb tense formed by combining the auxiliary verb *have* or *has* and the past participle of the main verb. (10n-1)

present progressive tense   A verb tense formed by combining the auxiliary verb *am, is,* or *are* and the *–ing* form of a main verb. (10n-1)

present tense   A verb tense used to express a general statement, make an observation, or describe an habitual activity. (10k, 10n-1)

principal parts   The major forms of a verb. (10k)

pronoun   A word that substitutes for a noun or noun phrase. (9a-2, 10a)

proper noun   A word that names a particular person, place, institution, organization, month, or day. (9a-1)

reciprocal pronoun   A pronoun that refers to the separate parts of a plural antecedent. (9a-2)

reflexive pronoun   A pronoun that consists of a personal pronoun plus –*self* or –*selves*. (9a-2)

regular verb   A verb that forms the third-person singular present tense by adding *s* or *es* to the base form, forms the present participle by adding –*ing* to the base form, and forms the past tense and past participle by adding *d* or *ed* to the base form. (10k)

relative pronoun   A pronoun that introduces a dependent clause. (9a-2, 10h)

restrictive element   Information essential to the meaning of a sentence and thus not set off with commas. (19j)

run-on sentence   Two independent clauses fused together without any intervening conjunctions or punctuation. (Chapter 11)

sentence   The basic unit of written language for expressing a thought. (9b)

sentence fragment   A grammatically incomplete sentence. (Chapter 11)

separable verb   A transitive phrasal verb whose particle may be placed after the object of the verb. (Chapter 24)

sequence of tenses   The time relationship among verbs in a block of text, expressed by verb tenses. (10o)

serial comma   In a series of items, the comma that separates the last two items. (19c)

simile   A figure of speech in which the writer uses one thing to describe another. (17f)

simple predicate   A main verb plus any auxiliary verbs. (9b-2)

simple sentence   A sentence that has a single independent clause and no dependent clauses. (9d-2)

simple subject   The noun or pronoun that constitutes the heart of a sentence subject. (9b-1)

subject   A noun, pronoun, or noun phrase that indicates what a sentence is about and typically precedes the main verb of the sentence. (9b-1, 11a-2)

subject complement   A noun, noun phrase, adjective, or adjective phrase that elaborates on the subject of a sentence and usually follows a linking verb. (9b-2)

subjective case   The form a pronoun takes when it is used as a grammatical subject. (10g)

subjunctive mood   A grammatical form of a verb used to express hypothetical conditions. (9a-3, 10h, 14b)

subordinating conjunction   A conjunction that is used to introduce a dependent clause and connect it to an independent clause. (9a-8)

subordination   In a sentence containing two ideas that are not equal in importance, making the lesser idea into a subordinate, or dependent clause. (15i)

suffix   A word part, such as *–ful*, *–ship*, or *–ness* that is attached to the end of a word—for example, boast*ful*, fellow*ship*, kind*ness*. (23i-2)

synonyms   Words that are similar in meaning—for example, *desire* and *want*. (23k-3)

tone   A writer's attitude toward his or her subject matter or audience. (14c)

transitive verb   A verb that acts on an object. (9a-3, 10f, Chapter 24)

verb   A word that expresses action, occurrence, or existence. (9a-3)

verb complement   A participial or infinitive phrase attached to a verb. (24f, 24i)

verb of state   A verb that expresses a condition or state, rather than an action or event. (10n-1, 24j)

verb tense   The form a verb takes to indicate the time of the action or the state of being. (10n)

verbal   A verb form that functions in a sentence as a noun, adverb, or adjective. (9a-4, 9c-2)

verbal aspect   The particular form a verb takes, within its tense, to indicate duration or completion of the verb's action or state of being. (10n)

voice   The form a transitive verb takes to indicate whether the subject is acting or being acted on. (10q)

Glossary of Usage

a, an   Use *a* before words beginning with a consonant sound. Use *an* before words beginning with a vowel sound.

accept, except   *Accept* is a verb meaning "to receive gladly." *Except* is usually a preposition meaning "with the exclusion of."

advice, advise   *Advice* is a noun meaning "guidance." *Advise* is a verb meaning "to guide."

affect, effect Most commonly, *affect* is used as a verb meaning "to influence." *Effect* is generally used as a noun meaning "result." As a verb, *effect* means "to bring about."

allusion, illusion An *allusion* is an indirect reference. An *illusion* is a false perception of reality.

awful, awfully Avoid using these terms to mean "very," except for in informal communication.

bad, badly *Bad* is an adjective. *Badly* is an adverb.

cite, site *Cite* is a verb meaning "to quote." *Site* is a noun meaning "place."

complement, compliment To *complement* is to complete so as to make a whole. To *compliment* is to express praise.

conscience, conscious *Conscience* is a noun meaning "a sense of right and wrong." *Conscious* is an adjective meaning "aware" or "intentional."

discreet, discrete *Discreet* means "tactful" or "modest." *Discrete* means "distinct" or "separate."

elicit, illicit *Elicit* is a verb meaning "to call forth." *Illicit* is an adjective meaning "illegal."

emigrate, immigrate, migrate *Emigrate* means "to move permanently away from." *Immigrate* means "to move permanently to." *Migrate* means "to move temporarily from one place to another."

eminent, immanent, imminent *Eminent* means "distinguished." *Immanent* means "inherent." *Imminent* means "about to occur."

farther, further *Farther* refers to distance. *Further* refers to time or degree.

fewer, less Use *fewer* with items that can be counted. Use *less* with general amounts associated with noncount nouns.

good, well *Good* is an adjective. *Well* is an adverb.

imply, infer *Imply* means to "suggest indirectly." *Infer* means "to draw a conclusion from what someone else has said."

incredible, incredulous *Incredible* means "unbelievable." *Incredulous* means "disbelieving."

its, it's *Its* is the possessive form of *it*. *It's* is the contracted from of *it is*.

lay, lie *Lay* takes a direct object and means "to place." *Lie* does not take a direct object and means "to recline."

moral, morale A *moral* is a lesson taught in a story. *Morale* is a state of mind reflecting levels of confidence and cheerfulness.

patience, patients *Patience* is the quality of being tolerant and steadfast. *Patients* are people who receive medical treatment.

peace, piece *Peace* is opposed to war. *Piece* is a segment or part.

personal, personnel *Personal* is an adjective meaning "private" or "individual." *Personnel* is a noun meaning "the people employed by an organization."

presence, presents *Presence* is the opposite of absence. *Presents* are gifts.

principal, principle *Principal* is an adjective meaning "foremost." *Principle* is a noun meaning "rule" or "standard."

raise, rise *Raise* is a transitive verb meaning "to lift" or "to build." *Rise* is an intransitive verb meaning "to stand up" or to "ascend."

real, really *Real* is an adjective; *really* is an adverb. In both cases, these terms should be avoided in formal writing.

respectfully, respectively *Respectfully* means "with respect." *Respectively* means "in the order given."

set, sit *Set* is used more often as a transitive verb meaning "to place" or "to arrange." *Sit* is an intransitive verb meaning "to take a seat."

stationary, stationery *Stationary* is an adjective meaning "not moving." *Stationery* is a noun meaning "writing materials."

than, then *Than* is a conjunction used to introduce the second part of a comparison. *Then* is an adverb meaning "at that time."

that, which As a relative pronoun, *that* is used only in restrictive clauses. *Which* can be used with either restrictive or nonrestrictive clauses.

their, there, they're *Their* is the possessive form of *they*. *There* is an adverb of place, it is also used in expletive constructions. *They're* is a contraction for *they are*.

threw, through/thru *Threw* is the past tense of the verb *to throw*. *Through* is a preposition. Do not use *thru* in formal writing.

till, until, 'til *Till* and *until* are both acceptable in formal writing; *'til* is informal.

use, utilize In most cases, *use* is the better choice. *Utilize* should be used specifically to mean "to make practical use of."

who, whom *Who* and *whom* are used as interrogative and relative pronouns (see 10h). *Who* stands for a grammatical subject. *Whom* stands for a grammatical object.

who's, whose *Who's* is a contraction for *who is*. *Whose* is the possessive form of *who*.

your, you're *Your* is the possessive form of *you*. *You're* is a contraction for *you are*.

Index